SEP 1 4 2006

Teach Your Dog to Read

Teach Your Dog to Read

A Unique Step-by-Step Program

to Expand Your Dog's Mind

and Strengthen the Bond Between You

Bonnie Bergin, Ed.D.

with SHARON HOGAN

Broadway Books • *New York*

BROADWAY

PRINTED IN THE UNITED STATES OF AMERICA

BROADWAY BOOKS and its logo, a letter B bisected on the diagonal, are trademarks of Random House, Inc.

Photographs by Bonnie Bergin, Jim Bergin, and Denis Getz.

Visit our website at www.broadwaybooks.com

BOOK DESIGN BY DEBORAH KERNER • DANCING BEARS

Library of Congress Cataloging-in-Publication Data
Bergin, Bonnie.
Teach your dog to read : a unique step-by-step program to expand your dog's mind and strengthen the bond between you / Bonnie Bergin.—1st ed.
p. cm.
Includes bibliographical references and index.
1. Dogs—Training. 2. Dogs—Psychological aspects. 3. Human-animal communication. I. Title.

SF431.B4337 2006
636.7'0835—dc22
2005050844

ISBN 0-7679-2245-X

1 3 5 7 9 10 8 6 4 2

First Edition

To *Keila* (my black Lab),
who expanded
my understanding of dogs' ability
to think,

and to *Nexus* (my white golden retriever),
who enlightened me
about dogs' ability to read

CONTENTS

Acknowledgments

There are always many people involved in making a book happen, but in my life none is more significant than my husband, Jim, who generously provides me the space, time, and encouragement to see my dreams to fruition. When we were first married, I naively inscribed a gift to him "My husband, my world." Thirty-seven years later, this truth is even more in evidence.

I need to also thank my dogs, Keila, Hoja, Angel, Harvey, Nexus, and Nugget, for their willingness to lie at my feet in silent support as I gathered my thoughts and efforts together to bring this book to publishable form. All are valued for their generosity of spirit and their willingness to pose for the photos herein.

This book could not have happened, however, without the turns of phrase provided by Sharon Cloud Hogan. I hope we have the opportunity to work together again.

My sincere thanks to Colleen Mohyde, my agent, who has kindly shaped my writing projects so they would reach my targeted audience: you. She knew how much it meant to me that these amazing capabilities of the dog be shared with others. To that end, she brought Sharon and me together, then invited Jennifer Josephy at Broadway Books to review the proposal.

I shall always be grateful to Jennifer, who saw in this unique work the potential I believe it holds: a means for dog lovers to know their dogs at a deeper, more fulfilling level. Learning is fun, and exploring the mystery of the dog's mind, expanding on his perceived capabilities, adds another dimension of zest in your partnership with your dog.

And last but not least, I owe a huge debt of gratitude to the board of trustees, faculty, staff, students, clients, volunteers, and dogs of the Assistance Dog Institute with whom I work daily. Through their efforts, many of my dreams have become reality. Their support and belief in my ideas is inspiring. I can only hope I have given them as much as I have received.

Preface

You may have picked up this book because of the irresistible dog on the cover. Or you may have picked it up because you heard somewhere that I'm an expert dog trainer who can teach some stupendous tricks.

If it was the scholarly puppy in the photograph that caught your eye, I know you will enjoy the many wonderful pictures throughout these pages. If, however, you went to the bookstore in search of *Teach Your Dog to Read* because you heard some buzz about my dog-training credentials, I offer you an apology and a confession: I'm not really a dog trainer.

Before you ask for a refund, please hear me out. I may not use conventional training methods to make dogs perform, but I do know a thing or two about how dogs learn. In truth, I'm a schoolteacher with degrees in higher education, special education, early childhood education, English, psychology, and social science. I came to the dog world not with a background in animal behavior, but as an experienced elementary, secondary, and college-level teacher.

In 1975, when I began to work with dogs, I was oblivious to the traditional dog training techniques of that time. I have since learned that most dog trainers were like canine chiropractors—they manipulated the dog's body to get the desired result. To teach a dog to sit, for example, they might put one hand on the dog's chest to physically restrain his forward movement while putting another hand on his butt, forcing it to the ground. When taught by these methods, with enough practice and corrections, the dog's body learned to do what the trainer asked. It was all about physical conditioning. His mind had very little to do with it.

My interest was and continues to be education — education that stems not from molding the body, but from expanding the mind. When I applied what I knew about how children learn to teaching dogs, I was blown away by their amazing cognitive capabilities. Again and again, I have witnessed dogs using their minds to figure things out. They can learn how to pull wheelchairs, turn lights on and off, pick up dropped or needed items (like a pen or pencil), open doors and drawers, and retrieve ringing telephones. When they put their minds to it, dogs can learn far more than they are physically "trained" to do.

In the 1970s, my faith in dogs' mental powers inspired me to start the service dog movement (service dogs assist people whose mobility is limited by physical and developmental disabilities) and Canine Companions for Independence (CCI), the largest assistance dog program in the world. In 1991, I opened the Assistance Dog Institute (ADI) to educate others about service dog training and other forms of assistance dog training and to conduct research into the most efficient, effective methods for teaching dogs. Today, ADI is the only university that grants college degrees (associate of science and master's degrees) in dog studies. Individuals come to the institute from all over the world to learn how to start their own or to improve an existing assistance dog program.

For three busy decades, my passion for teaching dogs has been fueled by their extraordinary capacity for learning.

From time to time, I have wondered if they, like people, could use their remarkable mental abilities to learn to read. Finally, when I had a free moment to try teaching them, I did.

That moment occurred three years ago at ADI in Santa Rosa, California. In December 2002, I shared my curiosity about whether dogs could read with Jana Edmondson, who worked for me at the institute. I gave her some basic directions to experiment with over the Christmas holiday. Jana wrote the commands *sit* and *down* on sheets of paper and showed them to her dog, a white golden retriever named Stock. With practice, Stock responded to those words!

When I came back from vacation, Jana told me about Stock's ability. Observing Jana and Stock at work, and experimenting with other dogs, I was able to put together steps for teaching dogs to read, and I began to show my students at ADI how to teach their dogs and puppies to read.

At first, we taught the dogs to associate words printed in black letters on white paper with verbal commands they were already familiar with. They learned to read quickly, and their abilities far surpassed our expectations. Soon, without verbal cues, they sat when we held up the flash card "sit" and downed when we held up the flash card "down."

Is this reading? Certainly, at the very least, the dogs recognized and responded to the abstract lettering that had taken on meaning for them.

Since then, in classes at the institute and in those that we sponsor all over the United States and in Japan, more than 350 dogs have displayed this capability. Some are even reading Japanese characters!

After we began to teach dogs to read, I started to think about the way humans learned to read 6,000 years ago. The first human readers interpreted picture drawings. These pictures then morphed into quick and versatile drawings of stick figures. In time, the stick-figure drawings turned at angles and changed to become letters of the alphabet.

As an experiment, I created computer-generated stick figures of dogs in different postures. We tested four dogs who had already learned to read *sit, down, turn, up,* and *roll.* All four responded to stick figures that portrayed these concepts *without being taught.* Astounding! I am convinced that dogs can reason, deduce, and conceptualize far beyond what we ever believed they could.

Even after thirty years in the dog business, I am thrilled by what our dogs have done and by what they are capable of doing. I hope that you will experience this sense of delight as you embark on the adventure of teaching your own dog to read.

IN DOGS WE TRUST,

BONNIE BERGIN, ED.D.
SANTA ROSA, CALIFORNIA

Introduction

*O*kay, you're right: Your dog will never be able to read this book. While she may have your keen visual ability to scan a written line, we have yet to know if a dog has the deductive powers to take in a page of text and decide that this book is fabulous.

To a dog, a whole page of text—like our spoken language—may be one big soupy blur. We do know that we can no more get a dog to enjoy the plot of a John Grisham novel than we can get her to respond to the command *sit* when we utter a sentence like "Iwantyoutosityourbuttontheground-rightnow." An adept dog who has heard the word *sit* many times may be able to sort through that verbal stew to find the one sound that makes sense: *sit*. Most dogs won't—for lack of understanding or motivation.

How then can we teach a dog to read? By teaching her one word or symbol at a time. In this book, I will show you how your dog can accurately respond to flash cards that contain a word or stick-figure symbol. Just as she can sit when we say *sit* or when we cue her with a hand signal, she can look at a flash card that contains the word *sit* and perform accordingly.

My method is simple: First we use the verbal command along with the flash card to help the dog make the association. Usually, in three to five tries, she will read the card with no verbal prompting at all. When she shows us that she can read—by following written commands to *sit, stand, turn,* or *kiss,* for example—we reward her for her efforts with copious praise and delectable treats. I have taught hundreds of dogs to read, and I have known dogs who have mastered up to twenty written words. In my heart of hearts, I believe they are capable of learning much more.

What's the Point?

This is not a joke book or a guide to cute tricks for circus dogs. It's a handbook to a revolution! Dogs are brilliant, perceptive beings who can sense the silent approach of a tsunami, sniff out the hostility of a terrorist walking through an airport, and pick up on the pain of a child who is in distress. They try desperately to tell us what they know, but we won't truly be able to understand them until we have a precise, reliable, two-way form of communication with them. Dogs who can read have a greater capacity not just to know what we want them to do, but to speak back to us in unlimited helpful ways.

For example, someday dogs may be able to combine their reading skills with their exceptional sense of smell to help scientists identify different types of cancers or other diseases. Dogs who are skilled at reading also can be indispensable to people with disabilities. A man with a visual impairment can say the command "exit"; his guide dog will first scan the walls for the exit sign, then lead him to the door. In airports and shopping malls, a dog who can read can find the proper male, female, or handicapped restroom symbol for a person who is visually impaired or physically challenged.

You may not need your dog to read for scientific research or because you have a disability. You may simply want to teach your dog to read because doing so will help you form a deeper relationship with him. Lately, for instance, I have been training my dogs to go to a posted reading card (such as *water, treat,* or *pet me*) to tell me what's on their minds. If you think you and your dog are soul mates now and you can communicate through eye contact and body language, you're right. Imagine how much more interesting your relationship will be when you can share written words.

We're on the forefront of a groundbreaking revolution — a revolution that has the potential to help dogs become smarter, better companions. Reading may be the wave of our future communications with our very best friends in this world: our dogs.

Are You Still Skeptical?

*E*ven if you believe that your dog can learn to read words from a flash card, you still may have doubts about why you would want him to do so. Why go to all of the bother of preparing flash cards and teaching your dog if you can simply open your mouth and say the word? Of the many answers to that question, probably the most obvious is this one: You're not always around to say the word at the most opportune time.

Remember those warm chocolate chip cookies that disappeared from the kitchen table? The Thanksgiving turkey for which your dog was very thankful? How about the time you came home and found your dog curled up in the fancy chair that he knows is verboten?

If your dog had been able to read the $\oslash$ symbol from a sign propped up beside your food on that chair, you wouldn't have missed Thanksgiving dinner and you wouldn't have dog hair on your pants.

Someday, at highway rest areas, dogs will be able to identify symbols of dogs in the universal pooping position; these signs will mark acceptable dog toileting areas. Likewise, they will be able to understand that a dog toilet symbol with a slash across it means "No pooping on this lawn."

If your dog follows you from room to room and you would like to be alone once in a while, a sign that says "wait" posted outside a doorway will keep your reading dog from crossing the threshold.

Reading dogs also can transcend their usual role as man's best friend to become teachers and aides. When they are allowed to strut their stuff in classrooms and libraries, they can inspire and encourage children who struggle to read.

Beyond any of these practical reasons, though, I love to teach my own dogs to read for the thrill of it—both mine and theirs. It's mind-blowing to witness dogs as they stretch their minds and embark on this major step in their evolution. Consider what an incredible leap a dog's ability to read is! In human cultures, reading has always been linked to greater brainpower; societies that are most literate tend to contribute the most scientific advances. Reading stimulates networking between different parts of the brain, and networking enhances the ability to conceptualize. Although I haven't met any canine Einsteins, it's possible that reading can likewise expand a dog's mind so that he is capable of more thinking and problem solving. Who knows where their growing minds will take us? Dogs who can read are dogs of the future.

Why Haven't Dogs Learned to Read Before Now?

*S*top right there," you might think. "If dogs were really meant to read, they would have done it long ago. Obviously people are meant to read and dogs are meant to keep them company on the couch while they read—right?"

Well, you're right about the fact that dogs aren't prewired to read in the same way that they are prewired to walk. But neither are people! Dogs, just like people, are not instinctive readers.

It's also true that dogs, as predators, are naturally much more attracted to movement than to static objects like flash cards. So are people! Focusing on signs is not a natural act. In teaching dogs to read, though, we can make their love of motion work for us. Schoolteachers know that the best learning takes place when children see, hear, and do something physical related to the lesson: If they've just heard a lecture about the art of Claude Monet, they'll remember his style of painting better if they're allowed to make their own paintings of water lilies. If they've just read a play, they'll know it best if they stand up and act it out.

Dogs are no different. They probably would be able to learn to read faster if the *words* were moving, like prey dashing across their field of vision, but the fact that written commands require *them* to move—to sit, turn, or take a bow—helps to solidify their knowledge. Once they move in response to those written words, the words become deeply fixed in their memories.

So if dogs can learn to read in spite of their lack of wiring for it, why haven't they learned to read before now? *It hasn't been necessary.* For the longest period of time, domesticated dogs have been backyard pets. Before that, they were real working partners with people in a more agrarian society. Today we've sanitized their existence so that everything is safe for them. They romp around in fenced yards. We feed them and give them water and for the most part they join us in the household. Even though they have learned to adapt themselves to us, they've never had a reason to read.

Until now. These days dogs are participating more and more in our daily lives. Where once they were lucky to be taken for a walk, now they accompany us to yoga class. Where once they were expected to help hunt for dinner, now some people look to them as exemplars of spiritual lessons. As dogs play a greater role in human activities, their ability to read may open other doors to shared experiences.

Dogs who can read are astoundingly good companions, but teaching a dog to read requires some work. Reading isn't a natural process for mammals, period. It's not natural for dogs—just as it isn't natural for humans. Even so, if people can do it, so can dogs; and if my dogs can do it, so can yours.

How Dogs Read

*D*ogs, like people, are learning machines. Still, dogs have somewhat less to work with than humans; where our noggins might resemble state-of-the-art computers with great gigs of memory, theirs are like the early computers with less random access space. In truth, although dog and human brains are similar, dogs have a smaller frontal lobe (the part of the brain where complex thinking takes place). We thus have to help them build on what they already know. We have to help them make associations.

READING PICTURES AND WORDS

Even though reading is not an instinctive activity for dogs, they can learn to read pictures and words. That is, we can teach them that a single symbol (like a squatting dog) or group of symbols (like the letters in the word *kiss*) represents a whole word or concept. As mentioned, early human reading started with pictures—think of line drawings on a cave wall. Early humans were pretty good at "reading" pictures of antelopes and amulets, but eventually they needed more than abstract symbols for their ideas and objects. Their world was teeming with things to describe, but their brains maxed out at memorizing about 1,500 to 2,000 abstract symbols—not enough to represent everything that they wanted to say. So, as far back as 3500 B.C., the Sumerians began to use phonemes (symbols related to word sounds) and logograms (letters) in order to translate their entire language into a readable form.

Dogs, obviously, haven't advanced that far. Because their brains lack a human language center, our spoken words carry limited meaning to them. Even if I use the word *sit* on its own when I ask friends to come in and sit down, one of my golden retrievers, Harvey, will not respond unless I address him directly. Then I may have to say the word more than once to get him to focus on what I want. Unlike other seductive sounds and movements—like the gentle hum following the opening of the refrigerator door or a fox sprinting through the field—words are not his passion.

If dogs could translate the sounds of our soliloquies back into words in their minds and mouths, this book might be called *Teach Your Dog to (Really!) Speak*. But no, alas, teaching phonemes—the building blocks of our words—would probably constitute wasted energy at this point in the evolution of a dog's brain. I would not fully discount doing so in the future, however. We are just beginning to discover what dogs are capable of!

HOW MUCH CAN DOGS LEARN?

Dogs *are* attuned to the emotional tenor of our voices, even if the dictionary meaning of our words flows right by. They also can and do learn to associate a spoken word to a specific posture or item, and they learn it relatively quickly. However, their vocabulary is nowhere near the 40,000 words the average person uses in conversation each day. Dogs, unlike humans who march down city sidewalks shouting into cell phones, "Can you hear me? I said tell Chicago to sell!," are not wired for multiword, complex communications.

That said, for almost thirty years I've been teaching a 90-word vocabulary to service dogs, and their vocabulary grows even more when they are placed with clients who have disabilities. Some of these clients say their dogs know more than 130 commands. In 2004, German researchers at the Max Planck Institute for Evolutionary Anthropology described a border collie named Rico who knows about 200 words—the same vocabulary size as apes, dolphins, and parrots who have been trained to understand words.

Twenty words for starters. We know that dogs can learn to read up to 20 written words, from three-letter words that represent the most basic commands, such as *sit*, to five-letter words that call for more dramatic responses, such as *shake* and *speak*, to three-word sentences, such as "Get the shoe." I was recently delighted to discover that dogs can read Japanese character symbols. In fact, at a seminar I taught in Japan, some students used English words and others used Japanese symbols. There appeared to be no difference in the dogs' responses. Nationality is no barrier to reading success!

Some dogs have learned to read up to twenty commands. I list some of the more common ones below. Don't feel restricted by this vocabulary, though. You may, for instance, have your own commands or words for these concepts (such as "spin" instead of "turn"). As long as your dog already knows the verbal form of that word, she can learn to read its written form. You can download these words to make your own flash cards from www. assistancedog.org/readingdogs.

Down: Your dog lowers her entire body to the ground.

Sit: Your dog puts her seat on the ground for a short time.

Stand: Your dog stands up with all four feet on the ground.

Roll: Your dog rolls over and exposes her stomach.

Turn: Your dog turns in a circle.

Shake: Your dog offers her paw in greeting.

Speak: Your dog barks when you tell her to.

Bow: Your dog takes a bow on command.

Up: Your dog puts her front paws up on the edge of a table, countertop, desk, or on a wall.

Kiss: Your dog gives you a quick lick on the cheek.

Go to bed: Your dog goes to her special bed or designated sleeping area.

And some stick figures . . . Whether we're talking about the Japanese character symbol for *down* or a stop sign at a busy intersection, we don't know how many symbols dogs can retain or how much they can truly understand once they begin to read. So far, some dogs who have been trained at our institute can read fifteen stick figures, and we are working on five assorted other symbols.

Of all the extraordinary surprises that I have experienced since we began to teach dogs to read, the most fantastic involved stick figures and my wonder dog, Nexus.

Nexus Makes the Connection

*F*rom a litter of white golden retrievers I saw in England in 2001, I chose two young pups. One we named Nexus; the other, Norton. Jorjan Powers, my public relations director at the Assistance Dog Institute, fell in love with Norton, so I took Nexus home to join my other five dogs.

The word *nexus* comes from the Latin word *nectere*, which means "to bind" in a connection or link. Little did I know at the time that Nexus and Norton would be the key links in our reading program—the dogs who made the leap from reading by association to true, freestyle recognition of the meaning of symbols.

Nexus was one of the first dogs who learned to read, and she had been a whiz at reading words on flash cards for some time. One day, I taught her to sit and lie down in response to stick figures of dogs in those positions. The next day, I decided to teach her to read a third stick figure—that of a dog rolling. I called Nexus into the living room to work with her on this skill. I held the card in front of myself for her to see, but then I was momentarily distracted by something in another part of the room. When I turned back to Nexus, my well-read dog was already rolling in response to the flash card that showed a stick figure of a dog upside-down! I hadn't spoken. I hadn't cued her with a hand signal. She had simply *read the card*.

I was shocked, so I tried another card. Now, *turn* is a fairly complicated command that calls for a series of movements.

The dog has to do a twirl in place. I had assumed that a stick figure would not be able to capture the movement and that Nexus would not be able to comprehend it. After a couple false starts, she turned, with no effort at all. In fact, she turned so fast I almost missed it. She was able to decipher my funny little stick-figure drawing. She was reading!

Reeling from what had just happened, I yelled for my husband to come watch. Nexus performed for him. I tried another card: a stick figure of a dog "upping" on a small table. Nexus upped. And so on. That was a total high, because I knew then that she was *really* reading—that is, making sense of a symbol in her own mind—without first being taught to associate that symbol with a verbal prompt. She recognized the postures of the dogs in the pictures and chose to imitate them.

If a woman and her dog could burst forth into song and kick up their heels together in a dance, Nexus and I would have done so that day.

Get ready to experience this same sense of exhilaration as you teach your dog to read stick figures!

How This Book Is Organized

*B*efore you get started, your dog will have to be up to speed with some verbal commands and you'll have to be up to speed with a few essential teaching techniques. In Part I, "Get Ready," I review commands such as *sit* and *down*, and I demonstrate how you can be an effective reading coach by building on these basic skills.

In this part of this book, you will also learn how to keep your dog's attention by using an expressive voice and a confident manner. Here you will discover how to prepare your materials, your surroundings, and your dog's attitude to teach him to read.

Part II, "Get Set," provides step-by-step instructions for training your dog to read his first, second, and third word from flash cards. Photographs illustrate this simple process.

In Part III, "Go: Read, Spot, Read!," I include steps for teaching your dog to read additional words. I also explain how your dog can move beyond written words to understand and respond to flash cards of stick-figure postures such as *sit* and *down*. In addition to these basic postures, he can learn to respond to stick figures of other commands and postures that he already knows. With prompting, your canine scholar can also learn to recognize signs such as the $\oslash$ symbol.

Last, in Part IV, "Reading Dogs Go to the Head of the Class," you'll learn how your reading dog can encourage children to read, and we'll consider the many other ways in which reading dogs can help people.

Dogs, like people, have varying levels of motivation, but motivation is the essential ingredient for all readers—fledgling and accomplished readers alike. Consider how much faster children learn to read if they're engaged with the story at hand. And consider your own motivation in picking up this book: Was it that alluring puppy on the cover, or were you driven to reach for it out of pure curiosity?

Most dogs are motivated by your enthusiasm, food treats, petting, play, and words of praise. Others are simply fired up about learning in general. Either way, you have to feed their motivation by making reading a stimulating experience. Throughout these chapters, you'll find troubleshooting tips that will help you work with a less ambitious dog.

Watching your dog read his first word is a thrill not unlike the moment when your child takes his first step, speaks his first word, or, for that matter, reads his first word. One part of this satisfaction stems from a sense of accomplishment; another part is associated with an appreciation of a loved one's potential. Who knows, after that first word, how many more will follow?

Part i
Get Ready

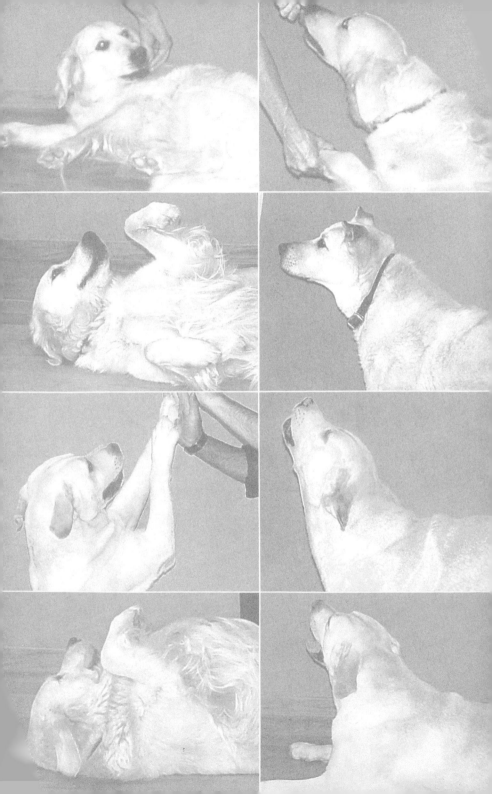

Learn to Be
Your Dog's Coach

*T*eaching a dog to read requires far more than a few flash cards and a pocketful of biscuits. This chapter will show you how your attitude and your dog's familiarity with basic skills can set the stage for successful reading lessons.

Expect the Best

*M*uch of what I know about how dogs learn comes from teaching service dogs to help people who have limited mobility. These dogs can learn to pick up things that are dropped, turn lights on and off, tug open doors, unzip clothing, and pull wheelchairs when their human partners get tired. Now all of the dogs who are trained at my Assistance Dog Institute learn to read, too.

One amazing golden retriever, Quest, works with Steve Sweeney, a man who has a physical disability and a brain injury. Despite Steve's slow, unclear speech and his limited movements, Quest does everything Steve asks without complaint. She has learned to be both versatile and adaptable: lying quietly beside his wheelchair during his college class by day and attending a rock concert by night. Steve has taught Quest to read more words than any dog I know: She reads more than twenty words and responds to stick figures depicting almost all of them. In addition to several commands that are included in this book, Quest sits up and begs, gets several different items for Steve, and can give a "high five."

Your dog, like Quest, is most likely smart and capable — she just needs some kind and consistent training. As you do your part in teaching your dog well, get ready to be astounded!

Can I Teach My Old Dog This New Trick?

Your old (or young) dog is probably more brilliant than you ever imagined she could be. Now, by teaching your dog to read, you are just pushing her training a bit further than you have before. Before we get to the bare bones of reading, though, let's dispatch with a question that may have been rolling around in your head ever since you picked up this book: Can *my* dog, my humble mutt, really learn to do it?

I've trained hundreds of dogs to read, and I can assure you that it doesn't matter if your dog is highly trained and smart as a whip or a happy house dog, a seemingly more simpleminded being. It doesn't matter if your dog is old or young, male or female. All can enjoy reading. Here is a tale of two dogs: Keila and Mac. Perhaps you will see a bit of your own dog in their stories.

KEILA: A DOG WITH BAGGAGE

My black Labrador retriever, Keila, had a nightmarish past with a family that treated her cruelly. She had been tied to a

tree and stoned throughout the day by kids passing by. At night she was untied and left to roam, to fend for herself, and to forage for food. Her heartbreaking story is, unfortunately, shared by tens of thousands of dogs who end up in shelters and pounds.

When I first adopted Keila, she would growl when men and boys approached her. Even though she was a smart, year-old dog, it took quite some time to convince her that certain behaviors were acceptable in the home and others were not. As a streetwise survivor, learning to "sit" on command was not as relevant to her as it was to other family dogs — she was still concerned about physical survival.

Today, thirteen years later, she is a strong-willed but affectionate member of the family. I love her dearly, and she me. She'll do almost anything I ask now, very seldom choosing to ignore or avoid my direction — but we both know she could if she so chose. That early streak of independence is still her safety net.

In retrospect, it's fascinating to identify the stages Keila moved through while adapting to life with me. She quickly adjusted to the feeding system, readily learning when and where food would appear, then gobbling it down as if it might not appear tomorrow. In no time at all, she became comfortable sleeping in the bedroom, a part of our family: my husband, myself, and our five other dogs. Housebreaking was a snap. She seemed attuned to the hum of the household. Yet one day she disappeared, leaving our ranch for places unknown. We were distraught. We trudged miles calling for her and regularly checked the local animal shelters. Four days later, she miraculously reappeared. Apparently committing to being here, she has been here since.

From that day forward, she was ours. She demands affection with unquenchable thirst. What I give her is never enough, but to her credit, she does try to earn it, looking to do whatever she thinks I require. Once she became more secure, learning to "sit" was easy for her. "Down," a posture of submission, took a little more effort, but she did it. Retrieving came naturally. Gradually a deep satisfaction settled over her.

She still gobbles her food, sticks to me like glue, accepts it as her responsibility to pick up whatever I drop, and expects affection on demand. In fact, we "argue" regularly about how much of me belongs to her and how much of me I am entitled to keep for myself. She usually wins. But now I can ask anything of her and she will do her best to figure out how to make it work. She takes joy in the doing, taking little notice of my recognition of her effort. She now finds bliss in doing tasks for their own sake, and she is self-motivated to learn. She is ready to read.

MAC: A PUPPY PRODIGY

Well-trained service dogs are astoundingly capable and flexible. They work for the delight of working, teaming up with their human partners in many ways in order to ameliorate the effects of their disabilities. Sweet, kind, and willing Mac is one of those dogs.

This large, four-year-old golden retriever with a very light-color coat was born into a different sort of life from Keila's. He was whelped at my house, and from his first day of birth, he was bused every day to the Assistance Dog Institute. There he met up with volunteers who come throughout the day to pet our pups.

At the institute, he also was matched with a student from the Sierra Youth Center. Through this program, incarcerated at-risk teens learn to train service dogs for people with disabilities. The youths benefit by learning to control their anger, to be loved, to use self-control, and to take care of another being. Mac benefited from a student's teaching. His formal training began when he was twenty-nine days old.

Mac was taught to sit on command by the middle of his fourth week. At six weeks, he was enthusiastically turning on light switches, starting to learn to retrieve, and responding to commands to "up" (put his front paws on a tabletop), go to bed on carpet pieces, turn, and lie down. For his efforts, his trainer showered him with appreciation and rewards.

Other commands soon followed, and Mac built a repertoire of ninety service dog commands well before the institute placed him with a human partner when he was only a year and a half. Learning these skills was a way of life for him from puppyhood. His exercises were carefully managed so that he enjoyed them, and his progress was satisfying for both him and his trainer.

Mac's early upbringing was as close to perfect as possible,

and so is he. He now works as a service dog, assisting a person with a severe mobility limitation. He constantly hears his human partner singing his praises, and he deserves every bit of it.

From birth, Mac's physical and safety needs were met. His lessons provided stimulation and recognition. While still very young, he moved from working for treats and approval to enjoying the opportunity to perform for its own sake. The more skills he has mastered, the more he has sought to master. Mac is ready to read, too.

YOUR DOG

A dog can never be too old. Whether your dog is old, like Keila, or young, like Mac, he probably can learn to read at least a word or two. We still don't know when a dog's brain is most fit for reading. At our institute, we have found that older dogs have a harder time remembering words than younger dogs do, so we try to start training our dogs as young as three and a half to four weeks in the hopes of building lasting associations in their minds.

If you have an older dog with whom you have a great bond, though, by all means go ahead and give reading lessons a try. In the end, the dog's personality and your connection to him may be just as important as the malleability of his mind.

Do make sure that your older dog can see before you begin to teach him to read. Some people think that their older dog is dim-witted, when, in fact, only his eyesight is dimming with age. You can tell that your dog's eyes are ready for reading if he is free of cataracts and he's visually tracking your movements (not just tracking sounds and smells) like a secret service agent as you go about your daily routine. A dog who can see is wired to pay attention to movement—that is the hunter in him. My dog Harvey, for instance, is alert to every move I make, even when he is dozing. I swivel in my chair; his eyes open and track my movement. I take a step forward; he's at the door before my second step hits the ground.

Because of their attraction to movement, it's easier to get dogs to respond to hand signals than to verbal commands. Using the dog's name to get his attention, followed by a sweeping hand motion, is much more powerful than just a verbal command like *sit.* We will make good use of the dog's phenomenal ability to focus during his reading lessons.

Another thing to consider if you have an older dog is whether or not he is in good enough physical condition to respond to the words that you would like him to read. My Anatolian shepherd, Hoja, knows all of the service dog commands, but she has been having a lot of orthopedic problems because of a cruciate ligament (knee) injury. Even if I ask her to do simple things like sit and down, it's very painful for her, so I've had to abandon the idea of teaching her to read more words.

A *dog can never be too dim.* About twice a year, I teach classes on cruises that cater to people with disabilities and their assistance dogs. During these classes, I often ask my students to bring their dogs up to the front of the room to demonstrate reading. Usually the dogs who have never been exposed to reading before "get it" after three to five exercises.

In one of these classes, a dog named Sam came up to the front of the class with his owner, and I led them through the steps that you will be learning in this book. We began with the flash card "down." Sam seemed slow in catching on; in fact, I didn't see a light in his eyes that he was getting it, even by the sixth exercise.

The next day in class, we tried again, but still Sam did not respond.

Finally, on the fourth and last day of the cruise, Sam did a reluctant down on his own. We were all thrilled, but wary. Sam's movements still seemed to lack enthusiasm.

About four months later, I was teaching on another cruise and Sam was back. I needed someone to demonstrate reading, and I asked Sam and his human partner to come forward. His owner looked shocked and nervous, because she knew how poorly Sam had performed on the last cruise. She showed him the "down" flash card without saying anything; he downed immediately. We were ecstatic!

Sometimes the problem is not with a dog's ability to learn but with his motivation to show you what he knows. Sam had to be convinced and to convince himself that reading was worthwhile.

Whether she is old or young, whether she has had a rocky start like Keila, is somewhat reluctant to learn like Sam, or has had lots of training and a sweetly satisfying youth like Mac, you'll know your dog is ready to read when you can see that he is eager to learn—for the fun of it. And you'll know that you are ready to teach your dog when you are ready for that fun to begin.

Breed is no barrier. Although I haven't worked with every single breed of dog, I've never seen one breed of dog that can't read. I have six dogs—an Anatolian shepherd, a black Lab, a yellow Lab, and three golden retrievers—and I have taught them all to read. I have also worked with a variety of breeds in my social/therapy and obedience classes, and every one is an able reader.

Some dogs, like terriers, are more excitable, and they may need to calm down a bit before they can learn to read. Others, like basset hounds, may need to get excited before reading lessons can begin. In the next chapter, I'll show you some tips for getting your dog into the right mood for school.

Self-starters wanted. Employers and teachers everywhere love to work with self-starters — people who take initiative and figure things out on their own. If your dog is a learning machine — eager to participate in new activities, with an active mind and body — reading should come easily to him.

If, in contrast, your dog is a passive couch potato, you may need to work with him to encourage him to think for himself. For example, at our institute, when a dog inevitably gets a foot or two caught in a leash, we don't thread it through his legs to fix it for him. Since many people with mobility limitations cannot physically help a dog in this predicament, he has to solve it himself — so we teach him to do so. We gently set the leash up so that he learns to lift his leg to untangle it himself. We do this with a simple tangle, then work with more and more complicated ones. In each instance, the dog has to figure out how to solve the problem. Reading is also a form of mental exercise, and if your dog has an agile mind, he is probably ready to read.

Be the Top Dog

To be your dog's coach, show him that you're the top reader of the pack. Just as the best elementary school teachers convey a passion for the written word, you'll need to bring your enthusiasm to the classroom. Maintain an expressive voice and a self-assured manner. Dogs, like people, are great at reading body language, so a coach has to be tuned in to his dog. Pay attention to your dog's mood and respond with just the right amount of enthusiasm. Gain his attention, but don't cause him to become so excited that he can't concentrate.

Follow the BASICS

*T*o be your dog's best guide and cheerleader, you'll also need to follow the "BASICS" of dog training. This mnemonic for *b*ond, *a*nticipate, *s*ynchronize, *i*nstruct, *c*oach, and *s*atisfaction covers the essential elements of a positive learning experience. Try to memorize these BASICS and keep them in mind as you teach your dog:

B = Bond. Dogs, like children respond best to those they love, trust, and respect.

A = Anticipate. So often the dog refuses to respond to a command because the situation is awkward or the command is too difficult to accomplish. A teacher can never be too prepared! Think through the issues that might arise with your dog before you embark on these training exercises. It just isn't going to work if a cat walks into view just as you show your dog the first word on a flash card. Read through this entire book before you begin. You may also want to memorize the steps of the exercises so that you don't have to flip back through the book in the middle of a training session.

S = Synchronize. A dog who is learning to read needs to be mellow enough to concentrate but energetic enough to respond to the written word. Since dogs naturally like to be in sync with their owners, it helps to exude both serious and positive vibes when getting a dog ready to read.

I = Instruct. Give a firm, clear instruction with trust that your dog will do it! Keep your facial expression calm and purposeful. Your voice should be strong, not emotional, and your command should be an order, not a question ("Sit!" not "Sit?"). Also, dogs tune in to things that are new and unusual. One of the ground rules of instructing a dog is to keep the environment and teaching style consistent initially (for instance, present the flash card with exactly the same motion each time), so the dog is focused only on the new information (the word or phrase) that you want her to learn.

C = Coach. Help your dog do it right! Encourage, support, and direct. Require a great performance. In both sports and dog training, the words of a coach can add gusto to the game. Throughout this book, I'll show you how to use the words *yes, no,* and (when encouraging your dog to read a flash card) *What's it say?* to guide her in the learning process.

S = Satisfaction. Just like a Rolling Stone, if your dog gets no satisfaction, she won't do it again. If she does get some satisfaction, she will do it again. And again, and again, and again! Dogs thrive on praise. Petting, ecstatic verbal and facial expressions, and food treats all make your dog's efforts worthwhile. In time, your dog will also take on the challenge of reading for her own sense of satisfaction.

The Key to Coaching: Develop "Two-Way" Communication

a good way to build a framework for later learning is to reinforce two-way communication with your dog. In

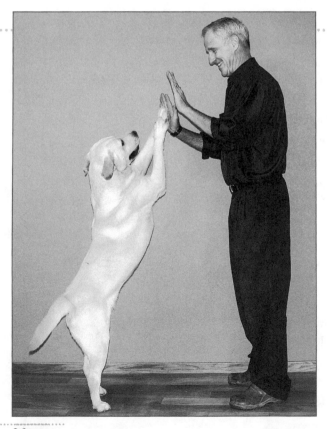

other words, you and your dog have to be in tune with each other. Without this sensitive connection, reading lessons will be exercises in total frustration for both of you.

GET YOUR SIGNALS STRAIGHT

Some no-nos of dog training can wreak havoc with this harmony. For instance, never call your dog to come to you in order to punish him for a prior offense. Also, don't touch your dog while giving him a command. Dogs, like people, are sensitive to touch, and touch will only confuse and distract them from the lesson. It is, however, perfectly acceptable to pat his head, rub his tummy, and give him a smooch after he has done what you asked, when you are praising him!

LISTEN TO YOUR DOG

Don't do all the talking—that is, listen to your dog so that communication is truly two-way. This may mean responding to your dog's "language"—his barks and nudges, his facial expressions and body language—in a way that shows him you understand. One summer afternoon, I came home after an exhausting day. My dogs, who were out in the yard, came into the house with me, eager to be petted. I left a puppy out front to play. As I put my books and papers down and sank into the welcoming embrace of the couch, my Anatolian, Hoja, who seldom "asks" to be petted, came over and nudged my thigh, just as I had taught her to do if she needed to tell me something.

"No," I cried to myself. "I need a minute to regroup." Hoja continued to nudge me. She started walking slowly to the back door. I thought it odd that she would want to go out when she had just been out, but I dutifully followed her. As I opened the door, I saw the little puppy frantically trying to stay afloat in the swimming pool. That's what Hoja was trying to tell me!

Having a good relationship—that is, being able to read each other—is essential before you can teach your dog to read words. Unless you can direct your dog to come and stand before you—to show up, as it were, in homeroom—the classes cannot begin.

Bone Up

MAKE SURE YOUR DOG KNOWS SOME COMMANDS

Children who are familiar with words from everyday speech have an easier time learning to read those words than children who do not know them. The larger vocabulary a child has been exposed to in everyday conversations, the more prepared he is for reading.

This is also true when teaching dogs to read. A dog will learn to read the written forms of verbal commands that she knows well much faster than those she is unclear about. Pre-learned is prepared! If what she is about to learn is similar to something that she already knows, she can make the association. Just as with a building, the foundation must come first. You can't build the fifth floor if the first, second, third, and fourth floors aren't there. You can't expand on something that doesn't exist. Make sure that your dog already knows the verbal commands that will be the foundation for her reading—and knows these commands very well. At the very least, ensure that she can down and sit when you ask her to. These exercises will be even more exciting if she can follow a few other commands like *roll, turn, shake, up, bow, speak,* and *stand.*

Make sure she can sit. If your dog doesn't know the *sit* command already, practice the following lesson until she auto-

matically lowers her butt to the ground whenever she hears
this command.

1. While your dog is standing, draw a treat from her nose
   back across her forehead while you repeat the word *sit*.
   Her natural inclination will be to follow the treat with her
   eyes and nose, which, when pointed upward, will cause
   her butt to lower to the ground. Don't hold the treat too
   high or she will try to jump up. If you hold it too low or
   move it too slowly, she will grab it. If you draw it back
   across her forehead too rapidly, she will twist around or
   move out of position in an effort to track it.
2. When she sits, give her an immediate "Yes!" followed by
   a quick thrust of the treat into her waiting mouth.
3. Reward her. The treat, a hug, or a pat, interspersed with

lots of "Good!"s that first time or two sets the dog to thinking, trying to figure out what she did that seemed so wonderful to you. When her mind is engaged, her learning is enhanced.

After a couple of exercises, you can begin to gradually withdraw some cues. As you say "Sit," hold your hand in the same position at the top of your dog's head—preparing to draw it from her nose back across her forehead—but without the treat. When she sits, say "Yes!" and give her a treat and pet her.

Next, say "Sit" and hold your hand up above her head, but don't draw it across her head. When she sits, say "Yes!" and praise her as you give her a treat.

Last, just say "Sit" without giving your dog any physical cues at all. Keep your hands to yourself. When she sits, reward her with a hearty "Yes!" and praise and treats.

Make sure he can down. Dominant dogs do not learn the *down* command easily because it is a submissive posture. If you've had trouble getting your dog to down, follow these instructions carefully.

1. Usually where the dog's head goes, the rest of his body follows. Take a nice treat and hold it between your index and middle finger with just a tiny amount of it exposed.
2. Show it to your dog; then, palm down, hold your hand flat to the floor as you say "Down." If your dog's attention begins to wander, gently pat the floor to keep his focus.
3. The flatness of your hand, combined with gentle patting, will encourage your dog to put his head on the ground as he tries to sniff, nose, and lick at the treat. Keeping a good grip on the treat, pat the floor less or not at all while you

continue to hold the treat on the ground. This will entice your dog to keep trying until he eventually lowers the rest of his body to the ground, flattening himself still more to keep licking.

4. If your dog's body fully meets the ground (not a second before), say "Yes!" and spread your fingers to release the treat. If your dog goes only partway down, and it looks like he isn't going down any more, go ahead and say "Yes!" and give him the treat. Some dogs need to be taught *down* bit by bit. When you do this exercise again, expect a bit more from him. Continue to expect a little more with each subsequent exercise until he is all the way down. If, after a few exercises, he really doesn't get it (and *only* if this approach appears to be the only option), put your hand on his shoulder and push down and back simultaneously at a 45-degree angle until he lies down.

5. Praise him!

When your dog responds eagerly to *down* for a treat, encourage the same behavior while weaning him away from the treat. This time, without holding a treat, point your finger on or near the floor. Say "Down." When he downs, say "Yes!," give him a treat, and praise him exuberantly. In subsequent exercises, continue to point, but begin to stand up, moving your pointing finger farther and farther away from the floor. Continue with "Yes!" followed by a treat and praise.

After a series of successes in which you gradually withdraw the pointing finger and bend your body over less and less, just say "Down." Stand straight and keep your hands to yourself. When he downs, reward him with a hearty "Yes!" and praise and treats.

BUILD ON WHAT YOUR DOG KNOWS

I believe that dogs know much more than we can tell, and what they can learn far surpasses what we can imagine for them. With our human-dog conversations essentially limited to body language, facial expressions, eye contact, and some verbal sounds (their whines and barks, our words), their response to our verbal commands is one of the few ways that we can access what they do know of our language.

When a dog learns a verbal command, she has to link it to something that she already knows. For instance, when you taught your dog to respond to the command *sit,* she had to associate the word *sit* with the posture of sitting. She already knew how to sit; your job was to teach her to do it when you told her to. To accomplish that, you first had to help her connect your spoken word with where her butt was supposed to be.

Teaching your dog to read works in the same way: She has to build links between something known and something unknown. The ultimate goal is for your dog to associate what she knows with a written command—without help from verbal cues. First, though, she must connect what she sees on paper with a spoken word that she is familiar with. Eventually she will build associations with the different shapes presented on several different flash cards. These connections in her brain will help her to become smarter!

The Rules of School

Rule One: Let Your Dog Figure It Out

*A*nother key to reading success is to engage your dog's brain in the learning process. The essence of good dog training is to get your dog to do, by himself, whatever movement you desire while you repeat the word you want him to associate with that action or posture. You can nurture this process along by being patient while he solves the problem, by feeding his natural hunger for praise, and by letting him imitate.

Let him hunt. For years, I was guilty of teaching dogs to sit by placing one hand on their chest to prevent forward movement while pushing their rumps into a sitting position. I wasn't letting them make the movement themselves. It was just like the way my dad used to help me with my math homework. When I ran aground of a specific problem, he would talk me through it while doing the calculations in front of me. When he did it for me, I could never get it and would have to traipse back to my bedroom to wade through it alone. I had to do it myself. And so do dogs.

Help your dog hunt for the answer and figure things out on his own. As he's staring at your flash card, perplexed and baffled, restrain yourself. Don't jump in too soon with the word as if you were watching a game of Jeopardy! Even if you need to give him a little hint, give him some time. He can do it.

Encourage his efforts. Even as you restrain yourself from stepping in too soon with the correct answer, you *can* provide positive input to guide and direct his behavior. With an encouraging, motivating voice, you can use the phrase "What's it say?" when your dog is trying to figure out what a word means on a flash card.

Praise is key, too. Of the ninety commands that we teach our service dogs at the Assistance Dog Institute, several (such as *settle, careful,* and *quick*) are called synchronization commands because our voice, facial expression, and posture deliver the message to the dog. We convey "praise" words like "good!" and "thank you!" with strong intonations, high volume, and delighted facial expressions. We send good vibes to the dogs and they try to stay in sync—they want to please us in return.

Throughout this book, I'll provide you with some specific ways to praise your dog. For now, though, just keep in mind the importance of always cheering him on.

Work with her ability to ape. Just as we can make use of a dog's quest for approval, we can work with her ability to imitate. A dog can learn to jump into a car by following another dog who already knows how. Dogs also can pick up even fancier skills. For example, I designed a room so that dogs can watch each other in training. One day a dog was learning to turn on a light switch while the other dogs watched. At the end of that dog's lesson, another dog was invited to start her session. The second dog ran right over, jumped up on the wall, and turned the light on! She'd had no prior training in this exercise; it was straight observational learning.

Just as dogs can learn from other dogs, they can learn by modeling the motions of their human teachers. A dog can even learn to take a bow by imitating a person who repeatedly models a dog's play bow position!

When your dog learns to read stick figures, she will be imitating the dog that she sees on the flash card. If the stick-figure dog is sitting, she will sit. If he is turning, she will turn. Imitation is second nature to your dog; keep this fact in mind as you teach her to read so you can put her natural skills to work.

Rule Two: Keep It Simple and Keep It Different

To teach children to read, teachers try to keep it simple and keep it different. Keeping it simple refers to the number of lines of text; the fewer lines on the page, the better: *Run, Spot, run!* Teachers also first introduce one-syllable words, such as *up,* which have short sounds and few letters.

"Keep it different" refers to teaching words (like *big* and *cat*) with letters and sounds that are easily distinguished from each other. Teachers of children who are learning to read usually don't put together words that rhyme *(Spot is hot)* or words that begin or end with identical letters *(How hot?)* in the same early lessons.

In teaching dogs to read, we are likewise careful about the words and letters that we use. Dogs, like children, do notice individual letters. We thus wouldn't use two flash cards that begin or end with the same two letters (such as *turn* and *tug*) during the dog's first reading lessons. Jana, one of my colleagues at the Assistance Dog Institute, learned this lesson the hard way with her dog Stock. When she introduced the words *turn* and *tug* too soon, he got confused, and months later Jana was still guiding him past his bafflement. She had to work with only one of the two commands for a long time, and only recently has she been able to reintroduce the second command.

Rule Three: Dance in Dog Time

I cannot stress enough how fast dogs learn. If something works, they do it again. If it doesn't work, they don't. And if they didn't get it the first time, they will the second or third. If you and your dog are up to speed on basic commands and training techniques, you know how quickly your dog picks up new commands and how difficult it can be to undo the damage from teaching mistakes.

Don't stop. That's why all of this preparation is so important. Once the actual reading lessons start, they move at an extremely fast pace. If you don't know the sequence of steps that the lessons contain, you might hesitate or need to flip back through this book while your dog is in a heightened learning mode. Because of these delays, your dog might end up learning an entirely different lesson from the one you intended.

If, on the other hand, you've got this material well nailed down in your own mind, you can prevent unintended intermissions in the action of learning. Read the instructions in this book in their entirety—maybe read them twice—and visualize and physically test out the movements involved before beginning the exercises with your dog. Doing so will ensure that your dog will have the best learning experience possible and might prevent errors that could mean long hours of remediation.

Take one step at a time. Dogs learn bit by bit; like human readers, they build their knowledge on a foundation of what they know already. Dogs who have had lots of training and structured interaction with their human partners will be more adept at learning to read than dogs whose primary interaction with people has been at feeding time. The first time any animal is exposed to something totally new and unusual—something that has little relationship to any prior experience—it will seem strange. With more exposure to the new experience and with more associations to similar situations, the unusual will become more usual.

Prepare yourself to set the right pace. Trying to teach your dog to read more and more words before he has the preceding ones totally committed to memory will only add to his confusion and anxiety.

Likewise, a good teacher needs to know when a student is bored out of his gourd and ready to move on to something new and exciting. Trainers sometimes unwittingly get into a pattern of repeating exercises and physical movements—all the while failing to notice that the dog "got it" already and is ready for a new idea. Always stop while you're ahead.

You'll know that you're ready to be your dog's coach if you believe in his ability to learn something new—and if you believe in your own ability to work with his many strengths. Get ready to interest your dog enough to engage him, and be patient enough to not overwhelm him. Finding the right balance will give your dog a real shot at greatness!

Prepare
Your Materials,
Your Surroundings,
and Your Dog's Mood

*F*or your dog to learn to read, the stars do not have to be aligned just so. However, heaven help you if you are an unprepared trainer, for instead of turning out a straight-A scholar, you may end up with an exasperated hound, a set of crumpled flash cards, and an empty box of dog biscuits.

To avoid this disappointing outcome, follow this chapter's directions carefully. You will need to laminate flash cards that have clear, clean letters (flash cards of words can be downloaded from www.assistancedog.org/readingdogs); stock up on fabulous food treats that are irresistible to your dog; and make a room reading ready—that is, spacious and calm enough for higher education. You will also have to figure out whether you and your dog are in just the right mood for school.

Stock Up on Supplies

*B*efore you begin your dog's first reading lesson, you will need to assemble some supplies. The tools of your trade are flash cards and treats.

Start with some simple, unflashy flash cards of the words *down* and *sit*.

The words. When I refer to flash cards, I'm not talking about the small index cards that you may have used to prepare yourself for an oral report in third grade. For these exercises, flash cards are large pieces of white paper that have been laminated to keep them clean and consistent. Large, thick letters in black ink on plain white paper work well. Don't use any paper that has distracting stains or smudges from coffee, ink, or drool. Keep the letters "clean," too, without fancy lettering, swirls, or serifs (the little lines that stem from otherwise simple typefaces). I have found that my dogs respond best to the contrast of dark letters on white, rather than colored, paper.

You may either handwrite the letters or use a computer. I've found that computer-generated letters work better than handwritten ones, but the difference is minuscule. It may well be my prejudice, not that of the dogs. I try to use the largest print size that will fill the paper. A Charcoal font with a font size of about 200 usually does the trick. (You are welcome to download and use the flash cards on the institute's website: www.assistancedog.org/readingdogs.)

The paper. Print or copy each word on a sheet of 8½ × 11-inch white paper. Be sure to write or print the word out across the longest part of the paper. This will make perfect sense when you progress to longer words: If you hold all of your flash cards horizontally, your dog will truly take his cue from the word, not from the orientation of the card. Be consistent.

Write the command again in the top corner of the reverse

side of the paper. That way, you can see which command you are holding up for your dog and you'll know which way to hold the flash card. (I have watched many of my brilliant human students holding the word upside-down!)

You may wish to put two 8½ × 11-inch pages of words back to back and laminate both together. You'll save a little money and it will be easy to keep the card right-side up.

Like children who often point to words and follow along with their finger as they read a book, dogs occasionally nose paper flash cards during their reading exercises. Their wet nose prints, though endearing, can crumple the paper. Laminating each flash card will protect it from wrinkling and prints and will help to maintain a consistent look to each card.

TREATS

In addition to flash cards, you'll need a good supply of food treats to attract and hold your dog's interest. As mentioned, dogs aren't naturally drawn to the static shape and detail of the letters on the flash card; rather, they are predators who respond to movement, scent, and sounds. Thus, the atmosphere that you create *around* the lesson will make the dog take notice. Appeal to your dog with the sight, smell, and promise of indulgences.

What are treats? Enthusiastic verbal praise, petting, playing catch with a ball, and bits of food are all treats. That said, not all treats are created equal. Dogs can and do discriminate between a so-so treat and a thrilling one. They match their efforts to the reward. Treats include anything that will bring immediate, intense pleasure to your dog. Adoration, stroking her chest, bouncing a ball so that he can catch it, a cheer, a big smile, and a bite-size piece of steak all qualify. The rule is, *noth-*

ing understated—match your treat with the effort you are asking of your dog.

Time and again I have had a dog/human team stand before me, with the human testifying to his dog's ignorance of a specific command. I then hand the person a tidbit of 100 percent beef brisket garnered from my husband's barbecue restaurant and ask him to try the command anyway. Usually the dog, now motivated by the food, follows the command in a heartbeat.

Once in a while, I see a dog who really doesn't appear to be interested in the exercise at all. In that case, I suggest that her human partner give her a bite even before giving the command. Never doubt the power of motivation! Just as with humans, for dogs there is a threshold between not learning and learning, and in order to cross that threshold, they have to be motivated. Feed your dog's motivation with treats.

I have also experienced the other side of the coin: Hard-boiled people who refuse to give food treats under any circumstances. They claim that their dogs are motivated enough without them. Generally those dogs are the slowest learners. They haven't benefited from treats that intensify the experience and speed up their learning.

Others say their dogs are so wound up with motivation that they run through their entire repertoire of commands in the hopes of finding one that triggers the treat. That can and does happen, until the dog develops a better understanding of the function of the treat. She needs to learn that she is to respond to the specific command of her human partner, not arbitrarily solicit for what she wants.

How food treats work. First and foremost, food treats should motivate. They also should help narrow the dog's focus on the learning at hand. These treats are particularly effective with dogs who are easily distracted or need an extra energy boost to pay attention.

In addition, food treats act as intensifiers as the dog builds associations. Again, just as a child will associate words on the page with words she is familiar with from everyday conversation, a dog's reading skills will thrive on repeated exposure to the association between one thing and another. One of the strongest ways to build that association is with intensity. So let go of the Puritan ethic—don't withhold treats (either pats or snacks) until your dog does exactly what you are looking for. Do just the opposite, in fact—shower him with treats so that he is completely enthusiastic and engaged in the learning process.

The logic is obvious. An animal in the wild will learn more quickly through an experience that either threatens or encourages survival than it will learn through a more mundane one. To really teach a dog, then, intensify each increment of learning and jackpot significant advancements.

Great treats—food treats together with your praising and petting—create this intensity. A ride in the car does not qualify because the treat is not immediate, nor does it allow for the exercise to resume where it left off the moment before. If you toss a ball, your dog will have to take time away from the lesson to run and chase it. Instead, bounce the ball right where he is standing so that he can catch it quickly and give it right back to you. Likewise, a big chunk of meat or a bone that takes time to chew will not allow the training to move forward in the next split second. To keep your momentum, think of small and speedily eaten treats. I have found that quarter-inch treats work best with my dogs because they can gulp them down quickly and get on with the learning experience.

Motivations change dog to dog and situation to situation. Some dogs just need to be petted after they read. Others just need a smile. You need to figure out what a great treat (that brings immediate intense pleasure) is in the eyes of your dog.

Set Up Your Surroundings

n ow that your flash cards and treats are ready, let's consider the room where your dog will become a reader.

THE TRAINING AREA

Provide enough space. Before you show your dog her first flash card, you will need to have room to back up and call her so that

she comes and stands before you. As her reading advances, she will need room to perform large motions, such as turns and rolls. I have seen trainers ask a dog to roll in a tight space and watched the dog get wedged against a wall or cabinet, unable to complete the move. Some dogs refuse to comply because, brilliant beings that they are, they recognize that there isn't enough room to do the maneuver. And their trainers think they are being stubborn! Make sure your "classroom" is spacious enough for success.

Have a place to stash your supplies. You will need a shelf or table nearby to keep your training supplies—the flash cards, treats, or a ball (if that's your dog's motivator)—within easy reach. Make sure that you can place the flash cards so that your dog cannot see the words they contain until the training exercise begins.

Remember, once the training sequence starts, the session moves forward at a rapid clip. Lulls in a session often teach the dog something not intended. For example, once your dog lies down in response to the "down" flash card, you must remove the card from sight. If the card is left in the dog's view after he completes the exercise, it will lose its significance. The association between the word on the card and the dog's response you worked so hard to build will dissipate. The dog will wonder, "Why, if that flash card says *down* and I am down, is it continuing to direct me to lie down? I must have misinterpreted its meaning." This would be the same as giving your dog the *sit* command over and over when he is already sitting down. The next time you hold up the flash card, your dog will ignore it. Instead, he will look for a different association. Avoid this problem by having a place to keep the words on the cards out of sight.

Dispatch with distractions. Other beings should not interfere with your concentration or work space. Dogs are naturally attracted to motion, so a child or dog who is diverting your attention or crossing paths with your dog in the midst of a teaching moment will impede the lesson. Worse, the interruption could alter what the dog is learning. For instance, you hold up the "down" card. Your dog begins to lie down. At that moment, your child bursts on the scene. You shout "No!" to your child. Your dog scrambles back up, thinking your emphatic "No!" had something to do with her downward movement. She will not be quite as willing to lie down again the next time you hold up that card.

Mobile kids and other pets aside, other distractions *are* welcome: smells from cooking, the TV blaring, and movement around the training area—provided they do not interfere with the training itself. We train all of our service dogs in a room with lots of activities going on so they learn to concentrate in a distracting environment. If you would like to take your dog to a school or library someday to show off her reading skills, and she has learned to read in a completely quiet environment, she won't adapt easily and may not read as well as she does at home. Dogs, like people, remember what they've learned best in the same context in which the learning took place.

TO LEASH OR NOT TO LEASH

Another thing to consider as you set up your "classroom" is whether to keep your dog on a leash during his reading exercises. That depends . . .

Outside of your home. A room full of other dogs in training (say, at a community center) or an outside area chock full of diversions (the scent of grilling meat, a rabbit in the woods, a child running by) definitely can make for a more challenging training environment than a quiet room—at first. Eventually, though, your dog will adjust, get used to the place, and be able to concentrate on his lesson with you. Later, when called upon to perform, he will respond comfortably in most environments. That's a wonderful advantage of training in an area where there are distractions. If you choose to train your dog in such a mildly chaotic atmosphere, you should leash him unless you can absolutely guarantee that he will not leave your side to explore other attractions. Slip the hand loop of the leash on your arm so that your hands are free.

If your dog is used to going outside whenever you bring out his leash, put the leash on him and take him around the inside of your house. Have fun with him and give him a few treats while he has his leash on. He'll soon realize that being attached to a leash doesn't always mean "out."

I don't recommend a retractable leash (with a plastic handle) for these exercises because you must hold it in your hand. Also, you won't need the long length of a retractable leash for these initial reading commands.

At home. Dogs trained in the quiet of the home do not need to be leashed unless they absolutely, positively, are not motivated by treats. Somewhere there must be a dog who, in the quiet and security of her own abode, will totally ignore my husband's brisket, though I've yet to find one. With something that mouthwatering in the room, there's only one place for a dog to be.

Still, if you have a dog who wanders off, unfocused and uninterested in the exercise, I would start by leashing her. Likewise, if she is distracted by every sight and sound—even with the most delectable treat offering nearby—leashing is a good way to contain that energy.

Nowhere, no how. Whether you're inside or outside, in a park or at home, never use a leash to punish your dog by jerking his neck with a choke chain or a flat collar. Rather, think of a leash as a simple containment system. If your dog chooses to run off with the leash attached, he will find himself struggling against an immovable object—you, standing firm at the other end of the leash. He will quickly learn that running off doesn't work. *DOG LAW: If it worked, I'll do it again. If it doesn't, I won't.* If, in the past, you followed him when he took off with the leash attached, your dog will have learned that it is *you* being contained by the leash, not *him*. It will take some time and practice to convince him otherwise. Hold onto the leash and don't give ground. Call him to you, and be patient. Reward him when he comes. If you are consistent, eventually he will learn what a leash is for.

Your Dog's Mood

Once your supplies and your training space are ready, you'll have to make sure that your dog is ready for school. To learn to read, she'll need enough concentration balanced with enough energy for her body to respond to certain cues. The tricky part of preparing your dog's mood is that you'll have to ensure that she's both aroused just enough to focus and motivated enough to respond.

That's why I've chosen *down* and *sit* as beginning reading commands. They are "downhill" commands—the dog's body has to make downward motions—so she won't need much physical energy and gusto. In fact, the amount of arousal that she'll need to perform the commands is in balance with the amount of arousal that she'll need to read. Even so, a naturally high-energy dog will have to be calmed down for this exercise. A calmer dog will require some hyping.

CALMING AN EXUBERANT DOG

Dogs, like people, have different temperaments. Even within families, there is a wide range of personality types; one person or dog might be very mellow, and another could make a cup of coffee nervous. Although people often generalize that some breeds of dogs (like fox terriers) are more excitable than others (say, basset hounds), within every breed there is actually quite a continuum of energetic to not-so-energetic dogs. If you want your dog to read, you'll have to go with what you've got.

Regardless of your dog's breed or disposition, how can you tell if he is in the right frame of mind for reading? Your dog needs to settle down if he is:

- Jumping on you
- Running around the room
- Barking excessively (not just barking to show interest in the exercise)
- Being playful and silly
- Showing too much interest in his surroundings

Never, ever try to restrain a dog in order to calm him down. Rather, work with him. Give him some time to investigate the space that you have chosen for training. He might want to run around a bit before you require his undivided attention.

To relax him even more, use a quiet voice and slow, gentle movements. Then do a little doggie massage until he . . . is . . . very . . . calm.

ENERGIZING A MELLOW DOG

If your dog is already in a slow frame of mind (or if your massage technique with your excitable dog was tremendously effective), you may have to fire him up a little in order to make him alert and motivated enough to read. If you suspect that your dog is too cool for school, you can be sure that you'll have to infuse some excitement into the situation if he:

- Seems lethargic
- Is lying down
- Is yawning
- Is scratching himself
- Has his eyes closed
- Isn't moving his tail
- Appears to lack interest in or focus on anything

Once the reading lessons begin, your dog may give the same signals if he is having trouble learning the information. If so, you'll have to make it easier for him to learn and be successful.

If your dog exhibits any of these behaviors, you might give him a treat to let him know that it's time to get ready for school. Smile. Running around the room, enticing him to join you, might help to jump-start his arousal.

Also, ask yourself if he is simply aping your depressed energy. Dogs like to stay physically and emotionally in sync with the strongest personality in the room. If you are the dog's owner, that's you. If you lie down, your dog lies down. If you get excited, he gets excited.

This synchronization phenomenon is a powerful dog management tool. If you're not enthusiastic, *he* won't be enthusiastic. If your dog is looking depressed, look in the mirror. Then try ramping up your own energy level.

Once you've revved yourself up and your dog has followed your lead, give your dog a once-over again. You'll know that he is ready to learn to read if:

- His tail is wagging
- His eyes are bright
- His ears are perky
- He is looking at you with focus and interest
- He is up on all four feet

A quick reminder: You, too, need to be ready for and engaged in the reading exercise. Don't make the mistake of some novice trainers: Tired and unable to shake the negative karma of an arduous day at work, they insist that they must train their dogs. The lessons that a dog learns from a trainer

FOLLOWING THE LEADER

If you have any doubt about the natural tendency for creatures to ape each other, consider this amazing example from my own experience. In January 2001, I was honored with the Angel Network's Use Your Life Award. Oprah Winfrey presented me with this award on her television show.

On stage, a tape of my training program with at-risk teens was playing for the audience and for Oprah. Offstage, behind the stage doors, I stood rehearsing my ready-for-prime-time smile (which is easily lost with nerves). When a producer gave me the signal, I walked onto the stage, reminding myself all the while to keep smiling.

There to welcome me was Oprah—as magnificent a presence in person as she is on the television screen. Radiating absolute personal power, she was at once both smiling and crying—apparently the film clip of teens training dogs to work with people who are disabled was quite moving for her. As soon as I saw Oprah, my fortified smile dissolved instantaneously into tears. What a moment—crying on national television—and I hadn't even seen the tape of my training program! The eyes of the leader had spoken, and I had followed.

with this attitude will require hours of undoing! You will have to be in just the right mood to make your dog a scholar. The rule in dog training is: *happy, happier, happiest!*

Once your head is happy, you can teach your dog her first word. Now pour yourself a cup of coffee and turn to the next chapter, where I will show you how to teach your dog to read the word *down.*

Part ii
Get Set

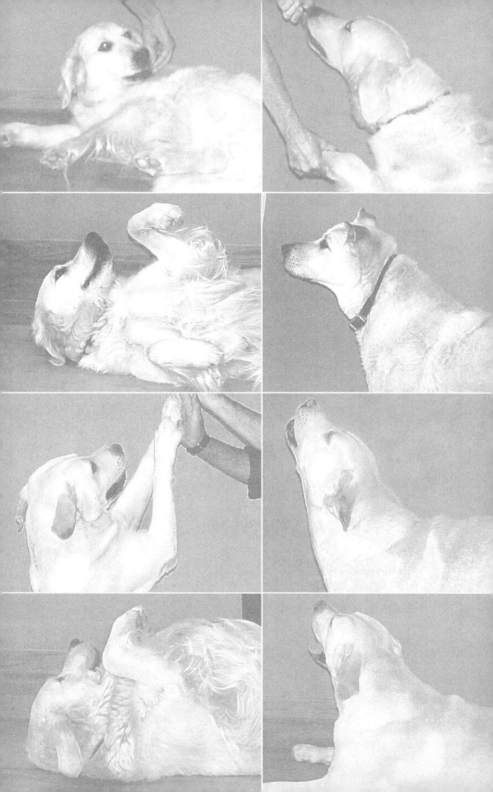

Chapter 3

Teach Your Dog
to Read One Word

*I*f your flash cards and bag of tricks (and treats) are ready and you and your dog are in the mood for school, it's time for the first reading lesson to begin. Follow the five-step method in this chapter and your dog will learn to read a flash card that says *down*, first with and then without prompting via a spoken word. Usually, after three or four attempts, a dog can figure out how the written word corresponds to the simple command that he already knows. For this first lesson, he must be able to lie down when you tell him to.

Why <u>Down</u>?

*M*ost dogs learn the command *sit* before the command *down*. You'll turn that order on its tail in this lesson: You'll show your dog the "down" card first. Once she really learns to read *down*, you can move on in the next lesson with the word *sit*. If you don't teach her in this order, your dog, a pattern detector, may assume that the "sit" card—and thus *all* flash cards—represents her most deeply embedded command, *sit*. Just as we tend to hold on to our earlier learned beliefs, so do our dogs! Don't let your dog get stuck in this familiar pattern and assume that all flash cards have the same story to tell.

Of course, while she's learning her first word, she *will* associate the flash card itself (along with the written word *down* that it contains) with the command *down*. However, it will not be as difficult to dislodge that concept when you move on to the second flash card, "sit," as it would be if you introduced the words in the reverse order.

After enough exposure to the second flash card ("sit"), your dog will seek out a pattern. Eventually she will catch on to the idea that the same 8½ × 11-inch flash-card shape can have two different meanings. She will realize that she can discriminate between one flash card and another by looking at the letters. If you had taught her the *sit* word first, she would have been less flexible in recognizing and accepting a different pattern on that second flash card.

In addition to the fact that they are the most familiar commands, I recommend starting with *down* and *sit* for several other reasons. They are both *discrete* commands; that is, they have a fixed beginning and end: With *sit*, for example, the dog starts in a standing position and ends in a sitting position. In contrast, continuous commands (such as *heel*) go on and on.

Down and *sit* also are *mixed-pace commands*. In other words, only one of you has to move to carry out the command: You stand still and your dog sits or lies down. In contrast, with *externally paced commands*, such as *let's go* (you and the dog are moving and the dog is walking casually beside you) and *step* (you and your dog go upstairs together one step at a time), you both are in motion: You have to concentrate on your movements as well as those of your dog.

Down and *sit* are good words to start with because they are simple, single-syllable words and because each allows for big (gross) versus refined movements, so your dog does not have to deliver a precise performance. Again, *sit* and *down* from a standing posture are both downhill commands that require less energy to carry out than commands that call for more acceleration and momentum, such as *up*.

Exercise 1. The Five-Step Reading Lesson

Step 1. All Paws on Deck

Pick up the booty. In one hand, hold the flash card behind your back. Put your dog's food treat or ball (if your dog would prefer to play with a bounced ball rather than devour a snack as a treat) in the other hand. If your dog is on the other side of the room, he'll probably show up as soon as he catches a whiff of what you're holding.

Everybody up. Your dog will need to stand in front of you when you show him the flash card. He may or may not be familiar with the *stand* command. If he doesn't know it, this is not the time to teach him. If he does know this command, *don't use it*. Giving one command when you are about to teach a different command can split both your concentration and your dog's. Just back up, coaxing him to stand in front of you. (Since you are starting with the *down* command, his sitting is not a crime, but for several other commands his sitting first could become awkward. For instance, some dogs will be less likely to respond to the command *turn* if required to get up from a sit to a stand, then turn. Standing will work for all of the commands, but sitting first works only with some.) Make sure that you have enough room to back up.

Also, your dog is always watching for body cues and hints

about what you mean. Be careful to hold your body still so you don't inadvertently give him cues.

Hands to yourself. Physical touch is distracting to your dog, so don't touch his body in your effort to maneuver him into a stand position. Instead, target him into position with a finger-point in front of you, a quick clap of your hands, a pat or two on your thigh, a call to him, or a combination of the above.

Get ready. Your dog should now be standing in front of you, looking up at you with his wonderful eyes. Prepare yourself to show him the flash card immediately or he may sit or lie down on his own, or worse, he may go off to investigate something more interesting than you.

Step 2. Present the Card

Ta-da! Bring the flash card to the front of your body, at your dog's eye level or slightly above. If you are tall, hold the card as low as you can (without bending over too much). Take care that your dog does not see the flash card before you move it into his line of vision. (You may want to practice smoothly presenting the card with one fluid motion ahead of time.)

Resist the temptation to make eye contact with your dog as he looks at the card. If he returns your gaze, he won't be able to concentrate on the word. To help him, keep your eyes shifted downward to the top of the card. It's okay to lower your head slightly, but don't bend your neck or body so that you are leaning all the way over the card.

Step 3. Speak

Down! Just as you bring the flash card from behind your back toward your dog, say the word on the flash card—in this case, *down*. Timing is essential! Your dog should get a glimpse of the word a split-second before you say it. If your dog is more used to hand signals than verbal commands, use the hand motion that you usually use for *down* with one hand just as you are bringing the flash card from behind your back with the other.

Step 4. Hold It

Keep the flash card still. If you move it, you will attract your dog's attention, but he will be attracted by the movement — not by the word.

Quickly check your position. Make sure that you're not covering any part of the word with your fingers. Look at the word that you printed on the back of the card to confirm that you are holding the card right-side up.

Hang on to the reward. As you show your dog the flash card, hold the treat in your other hand or leave it on the tabletop. This will help clue your dog to the fact that if he does what he is told, that treat will be his. Just make sure that the treat is not in front of the card. And remember: Don't shake your card, and don't shake your booty!

Step 5. Bestow Booty and Praise

Yes! As soon as your dog lies down, say "Yes!" in a relatively high-pitched voice. Clip the "Yes!" so that it almost sounds like "Yesp!" Doing so will help you to say the word faster. Say this word while you move the card behind your back or set it on the table.

If you use a clicker (see box on next page), click in place of the "Yes!" as you move the card behind your back or set it on the table.

Do not let the card linger where your dog can see it.

Just rewards. After you say "Yes!," offer the food treat with a word of praise, a vigorous pet, or all of the above to let your dog know how much you appreciate his effort.

Some dog trainers like to use a clicker, a small training device sold at pet stores. A clicker can help your dog know exactly when she accomplished the thing you were asking for. If, the split second she accomplishes the task, you tell her that is what you wanted, either with a "Yes!" or a click, you will enhance her ability to make the association.

Dog trainers do not always agree about whether using a verbal marker like "Yes!" is more effective than using a clicker. Depending on how you speak, a clicker may be faster than a word. In my opinion, a "Yes!" marker has one advantage: It can serve both as a marker and as a reinforcer. A "Yes!" that resonates with emotional enthusiasm when the dog makes a big step forward in her learning can jackpot her effort with intensity, strengthening the association.

Markers like the word *yes!* should be expressed in exactly the same way each time (but with a softer or louder intensity to convey your delight). "Yes!" is voiced in a mid to high pitch with the "s" sound clipped short with a silent "p." "Yes!" tells the dog that she did what you wanted her to do; she's on track. (Later, when your dog has a good grip on the concept of reading, you will introduce the "No!" marker. Wait until she is well grounded in the exercises before using this word, though, because its overuse could discourage her.)

Irrespective of the sound signal used, your dog must be clear that it signifies the correct completion of the task. You may use either the word *yes* or the click of a clicker when you are teaching your dog to read, but don't mark the moment using effusive words of praise such as "good dog," "great work," "wonderful," or "oh, Woofie!" These comments take too long to say. By the time you finish speaking, the dog cannot be sure which of the many things she did, including looking at a fly, counted for you. That ambiguity, as you can imagine, slows down the learning process.

You will want to use longer words of praise at the *end* of the exercise (after you have used "Yes!" to mark your dog's success). Just watch your timing: The "Yes!" is the message that the task is done. For the dog, that is the finish line. Saying it too soon would be akin to stopping a runner before the finish line to congratulate him, while other runners sail by to win the race. Saying it too late marks a different activity. Saying it just right defines the moment. Then your treat, praise, and petting follow, telling her how thrilled you are with her attempts.

Exercise 2. Try It Again

Once your dog successfully lies down when you say "Down" while holding the flash card, do the exercise again. The important point here is to go through the five steps *exactly* as you did before. Follow them in the same place, in the same sequence, in the same way. Don't go to another room, don't decide to try it a bit differently, don't throw away any of the context of the last trial. In fact, make a concerted effort to keep everything the same.

If the context changes—if you switch hands, bring the card out in a different way, or look at your dog's eyes instead of the card—your dog will have something new to learn. Then he'll be forced to divide his attention between those changes and the flash card.

When a dog learns something new, the first lesson is always an unknown. He is following blind. You have guided his success, but from his perspective, the fact that he did it is almost an accident. He really did not know what he was doing. He did lie down, yes, but he knows something else is going on. He just doesn't know what yet.

The first unknown bit in bit-by-bit learning happens in the

second step of the exercise (when you first whip out the flash card). Presumably your dog knows the room you are using for the lesson. He knows how to lie down when you give the verbal command *down*. In fact, the flash card is the only difference between this exercise and others you've done with him. Otherwise, the context is the same. Survival needs dictate that we — dogs and people — notice the unusual. The first bit he has to adjust to is that he *notice* the card. He can do it. The next bit is that he *associate* the card with the command you are giving him. The third is that he figure out that the card itself is a command that requires him to *respond*.

With this second exercise, it will begin to make sense to him — that is, if you don't change something. He will be able to narrow the scope of his focus, to hone his concentration on a smaller playing field.

A successful second exercise has the dog thinking, "Aha, that flash card must be part of this equation!" Remember, dogs are pattern detectors and pattern matchers. They are always on the lookout for links or connections to experiences. With the second exercise, your dog will be able to figure out "that darn flash card appeared again . . . just when I was asked to lie down. There must be a relationship."

When your dog goes through the second exercise, which is just like the first one, the flash card assumes weighty significance, because it is the only item that was unfamiliar to him before today's training session.

Exercise 3. Practice Makes Perfect

*M*ost of my students need to go through three exercises with their dogs before they can progress to having the dog respond without a voice command. Once again, go through the five steps exactly as you did in exercises one and two.

You may have to work at keeping your dog's attention on you and on what is to her a useless piece of paper. If she lies down on her own, turns her back on you, sits, stands sideways, yawns, looks away, scratches at her collar, or shows any signs of a lack of attention, your job is to bring her around. Clapping your hands while backing up works wonders. Of course, if the flash card is in your hand, clapping won't do. Call to her, make kissy sounds, or pat your thigh while backing up. If your space is limited, you can back up while you are moving in a circle.

Exercise 4. Skip a Step

*D*uring the fourth exercise, you will produce the flash card *without* the voice command. The steps now go like this:

1. All paws on deck: card behind your back, dog in front of you.
2. Present the card: Bring it out at your dog's eye level. Don't look at your dog's eyes.
3. *Skip this step; do* **not** *say the word!*
4. Hold it. Don't move the card, even though you are tempted to.
5. Bestow booty and praise: "Yes!" and "Whoopee!"

If, after you present the card, your dog hesitates and you realize that he isn't ready to go it alone, go back to Step 3 and say the word *down*. Try not to pitch in too fast—otherwise, you will prevent him from taking that all-important step of doing it on his own. If you wait too long, though, he may assume that the flash card without your voice means *to do nothing*. If

Teach Your Dog to Read One Word

you think that he needs a little help, just say the word *down* gently—make it more of a hint.

When you teach your dog to read, you may have to coach him along gently from time to time. If your dog hesitates at the same point whenever you show him the flash card without saying the word *down,* wait longer before giving him a hint. With a questioning voice, ask "What's it say?" Say these words exactly the same way each time, but increase or decrease the intensity of your voice. The purpose of saying "What's it say?" is to motivate, arouse, and keep your dog focused on the exercise while making him dredge his mind for the answer. Don't let this phrase become a pattern, though. Use it only when needed. If you immediately say "What's it say?" every time you hold up a flash card, you may be hindering your dog from following through on the exercise. He could be distracted by your voice and thus not read.

WHAT TO DO IF YOU HAVE A SLOW LEARNER

What should you do if your dog seems completely at sea? If reading seems like Greek to her, be patient and give it all time to make sense.

If she doesn't catch on at first, never laugh at her or show disappointment. Frustration, anger, and disappointment, just like praise, can serve as reinforcers, and you may wind up reinforcing a mistake.

Remain enthusiastic and try a couple more times before you present the flash card *without* the verbal command again. Be sure to wait long enough for her to give it the old college try. If she still doesn't perform without prompting, do say the word again, but without any obvious awkwardness, so she won't feel like a failure. Then, when she responds to the verbal command, reward her with enthusiasm. Always end on a positive note.

Wait until the next day to try again.

If you and your dog succeeded in the first three exercises —
that is, if he downed when he saw the word (as you were saying the word) *down* — you probably won't need to say the word
down at all during the fourth exercise. If you had less success the
first three times around, your dog probably wasn't sure of the
verbal command to begin with. Work on his foundation of basic spoken commands before trying the reading exercises
again.

Congratulations

CELEBRATE!

Every exercise should culminate with a sincere sense of satisfaction that makes the dog's effort worth repeating. *DOG'S
LAW: If it works, I'll do it again. If it doesn't, I won't!*

Even if he just did a bit of the exercise (like starting to lie
down but not going all the way down), that bit still deserves
recognition. Reading is hard work! Just ask any beginning
reader. By praising him for his response, even if it is only an
increment of what you were looking for, he will see that he is
on track.

Deliver that "Yes!," provide that food treat, praise, and
pet! Give treats, but not just any treats. great treats!
Souped-up love, delectable bites of food, exuberant petting,
smiles that stretch from ear to ear, hyped attitudes, and sincere praise all build lasting associations.

Over the years, I have seen many dogs enjoy the role of
service dog: picking up dropped items, tugging open doors,
and pulling wheelchairs for the pure pleasure of it. As our
skill in teaching reading and our dogs' experience with it increases, I've no doubt that reading someday will provide
them with a similar form of satisfaction.

In the meantime, your dog's sense of accomplishment

must come from your approval and appreciation of a job well done—particularly with beginning reading.

Dogs love, need, and crave emotion in any form they can get it. Charged feelings (preferably positive) reinforce behavior. Training with pleasurable interactions results in a dog eager to have that leash connected to her collar, enthusiastically looking forward to the next exercise, *ready to learn.*

Even as you shower your dog with praise, be very careful to keep your expectations in check; allow your dog to learn at her own pace and in her own way. Then you, too, will experience a sincere sense of satisfaction as your expectations match her ability to learn. This is a win-win situation.

HOLD THAT HIGH NOTE

End on a positive note, and plan to resume tomorrow. Limit each day's training to about six to nine exercises (no more than fifteen minutes total) with each flash card. With young pups, do even less (no more than seven minutes of training—including reading). More than that will lead to doggie burnout.

WHOOPEE!

Your dog just read the word *down*—or at least your dog associated the flash card with the command *down.* Since before today your dog's mental pages were blank regarding reading, a flash card—any flash card—will forever trigger that association. Read on to discover how to build your dog's reading repertoire beyond a single word.

Chapter 4

Teach Your Dog to Read a Second and Third Word

*I*f your dog can successfully read the word *down,* he is ready to take on the challenge of a second and third word. By "successfully," I mean that your dog has accurately responded to the flash card *without a verbal prompt* three out of five times. If he has done this, he is ready.

Most dogs are ready to learn the next word immediately after learning the first; sometimes the process can take a couple of days. You know your dog best, but try to strike a healthy balance between boredom and burnout.

This chapter covers the techniques that have worked for me and my students as we have helped dogs achieve a breakthrough realization: All flash cards are not created equal! It also includes strategies for knowing when every dog has had his day—that is, when too much of a good reading thing may lead to diminishing returns.

Once again, the sequence of teaching goes fast, so I suggest that you read through this chapter once or twice to prepare yourself before you continue working with your dog.

Also, remember that for your dog to truly absorb a new idea, to "get it," the concept needs to be more than a one-dimensional black word printed on a sheet of white paper. It must be a vibrant, delicious experience that the learner can participate in! Visual, auditory, and sensory inputs are all important in building lasting connections. Help your dog connect the dots between what he already knows and what you are teaching him by making his new associations intense and rewarding. Keep those biscuits and bites of beef coming.

The Word Sit, Day One

*T*he next word that we introduce after *down* is *sit*. At this point, you will be asking your dog to discriminate between two flash cards. This is the true beginning of reading. Your dog must look at the individual letters on the cards, not just at the cards as a whole.

Step 1. All Paws on Deck

*J*ust as you did when you showed your dog how to read her first word, make sure your supplies, your surroundings, and you and your dog are ready. Begin by placing the "sit" flash card behind your back.

Your dog undoubtedly now knows that if she responds to your request, a food treat is forthcoming. The booty can thus be left on the shelf or in a treat bag, or you might still hold it in your hand. If your dog is not strongly motivated, holding it in your hand might be more inspiring.

Say your dog's name or whatever you normally do to make your dog look at you. Sometimes it pays to give your dog a treat to thank her for her attention. Without giving a specific command, get her to stand in front of you. Again, you may need to back up a step to draw her toward you.

Step 2. Present the Card

*M*ost dogs won't thoughtfully discriminate between your verbal commands *down* and *sit*. Instead, they are pattern matchers—they tend to follow patterns they are already familiar with. You flashed a card and asked for "Down" last time. In your dog's mind, that must be what you mean this time. Count on her to expect to down even though you say "Sit." You must be poised to stop that from happening.

Bring out the flash card that says "sit." Your dog now has a pattern of lying down when a flash card is brought into view, so you'll need to be quick with this, or she will lie down before you know it. Keep in mind that you do not want to introduce the word *no* or any negatives in these early exercises so as not to discourage her early learning. The onus is on you to speed up.

Step 3. Speak

*I*f she does start to lie down before you are able to get the flash card into place and say the word *sit*, no problem. Simply take a step or two back while calling your dog to you. She will get up and move toward you. Now bring the flash card forward at her eye level or slightly above, followed a split second later by the verbal command *sit*.

Step 4. Hold It

*M*ake sure the flash card is upright, but do not move it around. I think humans instinctively know that movement is appealing to dogs, and I've noticed that most people tend to move the card without even knowing that they're doing it. If you don't hold the card still, however, your dog will

Teach Your Dog to Read a Second and Third Word

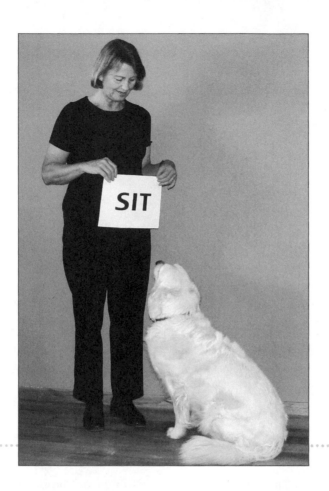

take meaning from the movement of the card, not from the written word, and that's not true reading.

Remember to avoid eye contact with your dog as she looks at the card. If she's looking up at you, she won't focus on the word. Instead, look down at the top of the card. You may bend your neck just a bit, but don't crane it or your body such that you are leaning all the way over the card.

Step 5. Bestow Booty and Praise

*M*ost dogs sit before downing, so you have a split second to say "Yes!" while she is in the sit position readying herself to slide on down. Do your best to stop her from downing at all or you will have to "unteach" it later. Since she knows that "Yes!" or a click means she has accomplished what you want, she will hesitate in that semi-sit position. Give her the treat immediately following an emphatic "Yes!" Remember: This is bit-by-bit learning—accept less than perfection.

*I*f your dog does manage to lie down, back up and call her to you as you continue to hold the card in front of her. Repeat the verbal command or hand signal two or three times to help her build the association between the command and the card. And again, try to say that "Yes" before she downs.

REMOVE THE CARD
Move the flash card behind your back or set it on the table. Do not let the card linger where your dog can see it after she has complied.

REWARD HER
Immediately give your dog the food treat, praise, and pet her. In two or three tries, she will make the association between the flash card word *sit* and putting her bottom to the ground. If she did sit without trying to lie down, congratulations!

REPEAT
After that first success, repeat the exercise. Do the exercise two or three more times to help solidify the sit. You are estab-

lishing associations, and you want them to be fairly deeply embedded in your dog.

ALL FLASH CARDS ARE NOT CREATED EQUAL: TEACH THE DIFFERENCE BETWEEN *DOWN* AND *SIT*

Mix it up. Your dog is now reading the word *sit* with aplomb. She has done it three out of the last five times you showed her the flash card. Now it's time to really shake things up—it's time to present the flash card for "down" again. Without breaking stride, giving no cue that change is imminent, show her the word *down* (without saying the word *down*).

Most dogs respond correctly by lying down. They get it! They can discriminate between the two words. If your dog can do this, mark the moment with a resoundingly positive "Yes!" Then reward her with praise and food treats. My congratulations to you, too!

It* was *something that you said. When I teach my college students, I tell them it is always the teacher (me), and never the students (them), if they don't "get it" because somehow I didn't reach them. Likewise, if your dog isn't catching on to reading, consider the way you are teaching her. Never blame your dog, but look at your own technique in relation to her personality.

If your dog did *not* discriminate between the words *sit* and *down*, practice with each card a couple more times. Help out with verbal cues if necessary. End on a positive note, and plan to resume tomorrow. Limit each day's training to about six to nine exercises with each card. With young pups, do even less.

Stop while you're ahead. Success can be its own worst enemy. A dog who builds more skills and associations with each drill is a dream to train. The trainer, seeing the progress, gets so caught up in his own desire for additional success that he is blind to the fact that the dog is getting fried with that exercise. The trainer keeps pushing the dog for more. The dog has no more to give, leaving the trainer disappointed and the dog feeling like a failure. The next day, the dog avoids that particular exercise. How much clearer can it be? (Often the dog still looks enthusiastic, but he is actually burning out inside.)

If you end the day's exercise on an upbeat note before your dog is exhausted, overnight his mind will filter out his mistakes. John Steinbeck said, "It is a common experience that a problem difficult at night is resolved in the morning after the committee of sleep has worked on it." Let your dog sleep on it! A night's rest can help to solidify the correct approach and make the next day's performance better than the day before.

The Word Sit, Day Two

REINFORCE YESTERDAY'S LESSON

Overnight learning is an awe-inspiring phenomenon. While sleeping, the brain sorts through the previous day's experiences, organizing and coalescing its lessons, particularly those accompanied by intensity. Oftentimes the dog is better at an exercise on day two than she was on day one. The lesson on day two will develop her ability to discriminate between the flash cards "sit" and "down" even more.

PREPARE MOUTHWATERING TREATS

Generally, the higher the bar, the better your treat needs to be. You will now be asking your dog to identify and differentiate *sit* from *down* more often than by chance. You will be randomly offering the flash cards for her response; for example: sit, sit, down, down, down, sit.

For this exercise, your dog will have to fine-tune her hard-wiring for pattern detection and make a serious effort to discriminate one word from another on flash cards. She can do it, but it is hard work, and the relevancy to her comes from treats. If you want to see a quality effort, make that treat worth her while.

Once again, you can use intensity to build associations in relatively short periods of time. Intensity can speed up the learning process, reducing the need for practice exercises. How? At each successful step, build a lasting impression and

KNOW HOW TO SAY "NO"

Since your dog has had prior successes with the flash cards (or you wouldn't be trying this exercise), you can now introduce the word *no*. When you use *no* in an educational environment, offer it as information, not as punishment. A firm "No" should not sound threatening, angry, frustrated, or disappointed. Use it to inform, redirect, and guide. If you say it quickly but kindly, with the word clipped similarly to "Yes!" with its silent "p," "No" sounds almost like "Nope" with the "p" silent. I recommend abbreviating the "No" in this way in order to make the word as short and fast as possible. Without consciously clipping the word like this, some people tend to drag out the "Noooooooo." Not good.

Now, when you flash the "sit" card and your dog begins to lie down, an informative "No" should redirect his assumption. If, during the course of this more trying series of exercises, he opts to quit by scratching, yawning, turning away, acting lethargic, or playing, an informative "No" coupled with really great treats should rekindle his interest.

You can also use the sentence "What's it say?" when your dog starts to fade or seems doubtful as to what his next move should be. This phrase provides encouragement and motivation to get him thinking and trying.

a strong association with the moment, the circumstance, and the motor skill. Reward her with marvelous treats and plentiful affection.

KEEP APPLAUDING HER EFFORT

Again, aside from the promise of treats in your hand, these exercises are not for their own sake relevant to your dog. I cannot overstate your role as the coach and cheering section. In fact, if an audience is available, ask them to clap and cheer, too. Most dogs respond well to applause.

Word Three, Day Three

*A*fter another overnight, your dog will be ready to learn a third flash-card command.

GET READY

If your dog reads only one word, she will associate the flash card itself with that word. If she reads only two words, she can choose one of two postures, and if she doesn't hear a quick "Yes!," she will realize that you are asking for the other behavior, by process of elimination. I have watched dogs, when confronted with a flash card, get into a down position, look at their owner, and come back up into a sit without needing to discriminate between the written words.

When you teach your dog more words, she has to pay attention because guesswork or the process of elimination no longer works. She has to discriminate. *Down* starts with a "d" and is four letters long. *Sit* starts with an "s" and is three letters long. *Stand* starts with an "s" and, unlike *sit,* is five letters. *Roll* starts with an "r," but is four letters. Some attentive dogs don't need to learn a third word in order for them to discriminate between words, but others don't really begin to read until you introduce them to a third word.

Which command? For the third word, I recommend *stand*. Standing and walking do require more energy than sinking to the floor, but the difference is minuscule for the dog with average energy, and these commands may be easier than sitting and lying down for the high-energy dog.

Next, you could introduce a *downhill, discrete, mixed-pace* command such as *roll* (your dog lies down, turns over, and exposes her stomach).

Don't get too carried away in your choice. Whatever you choose absolutely needs to be a command your dog does well with verbal or hand signal instruction.

No props. As you advance in the number of words your dog responds to, do not attempt to teach your dog a command (such as *up* [on a table edge]) that requires a prop. With such commands, repositioning yourself near the prop will be a dead giveaway. The dog will not respond independently to the flash card. You can teach your dog to read these commands when she is very adept at reading other words.

The same might hold true of *go to bed, tug, leave it, crate* (the dog goes into her crate), or *get the (shoe, ball, etc.).* Unless props like a table, dog bed, crate, and an item for the dog to retrieve or tug are always a part of your training area or room, moving the equipment in to practice with your dog will cue her to its intended use.

Don't move. Commands like *kiss* (the dog licks your cheek) present another problem. If you stand while giving the dog all other commands, but you sit before holding up a flash card that says *kiss,* your dog will respond to your posture rather than the flash card. If you are already sitting down, but you present your cheek for a kiss, your hint will decrease the learning opportunity.

Dogs aren't the only ones who give such physical cues precedence over the written word. One class of schoolchildren learned to associate the first flash card they saw to its correct written word. In addition to the word, this card had a thumbprint on it. The children then assumed that every other flash card with a thumbprint was that same word; they totally overlooked the fact that the lettering on subsequent flash cards was entirely different! Cards with a thumbprint, a phenomenon of nature, created a stronger association than cards with letters, which are man-made creations. You can bet that a dog, like the children, will first jump at an opportunity to detect a natural pattern like your body language, facial expression, or a crate brought into a room just before a flash card is shown, before turning to the written word for that information. For the same reason, beware of unconsciously trying to help your dog by giving suggestions through your eye or head movement or other body language cues.

Stick to the program. When you introduce the third word, you will use the same teaching method that you used for the first two words. Then, before merging the word into a random mix with the other two words, make sure that your dog has read and responded to it correctly in three of the last five exercises.

CONSIDER THE INFLUENCE OF PRIOR TEACHING
Your dog's response to your introduction of the third word will depend in many ways on how you handled the first two words. Her misperceptions and your awkward movements while teaching the first two words were counterbalanced by

the novelty of the experience. Now that she is catching on, this third word will refine the experience, defining it as a true reading exercise. Therefore, your enthusiasm, speed, and agility in teaching the third word are critical.

One definition of an expert is that his perception is better, his movement is quicker, and he has a larger store of alternative techniques to call on than a novice. My husband and I designed and built our last two homes. He enjoys saying: "Sell the first home you build to a stranger, the second to a friend, and keep the third for yourself."

Dog training is different in that most of us live with our mistakes. The upside is that most dogs are willing to forgive us for our transgressions. Some will even try to overlook them — allowing the new way to overshadow the old. Although once an association is sent to the memory, it is stored there forever (and a stressful event could cause it to be recalled), in general, the memory of a mistake will fade with time.

TEACH THE THIRD WORD

Expect more of yourself and less of your dog. You can learn from *your* mistakes, so introduce the third word by using the same techniques that you used in teaching the first two words, but do them better. However, do not raise your expectations of your dog. In fact, expect less. She is on her third word. Her brain is stretched, and reading is not a novelty anymore. Of and by itself, the exercise is no longer new and intense. In fact, because her pages are no longer blank, you will need to instill a higher sense of purpose and excitement.

With some dogs, that stretching of the brain is accompanied by barking, almost as if they are expressing their frustration at the difficulty of the exercise. If your dog does this, don't insist that she stop barking, or you will divert her attention. Just ignore it and continue with the exercise.

Set the mood. Your dog now knows that a wonderful food treat and an armload of your enthusiasm follow each effort. That may be enough incentive for some dogs to jump willingly into this next stage of reading. In fact, some may exhibit this gusto with a display of their entire command repertoire: sit, down, roll, up, turn, bow, and so forth. Please understand that if this does occur, your dog is not being a wiseass. She is offering what she knows in the hopes of pleasing you. Your smile is a reward. So don't smile. Instead, stay calm and with a serious expression say "No." Translated, this means "Quit the circus performance."

Other dogs may be less physically active and upbeat by the time you are ready to introduce the third word. You will need to counteract that lethargy with synchronization. Infuse your dog with your infectious energy and enthusiasm for the upcoming exercises. Remember, as a trainer-coach, you are the orchestra leader, increasing and decreasing arousal as needed at each stage of the performance.

Beware of burnout. Unfortunately, some dogs will not respond well to the third word even if you stand on your head. The strongest clue that you did too many exercises with your dog the day before is not her loss of interest that day, but rather her lack of interest the *next* day. Overnight learning filtered out her sense of enthusiasm in favor of remembering her sense of burnout from exercise after exercise after exercise.

Through the years, I've paid the price for putting too much pressure on dogs during training. Once, one of our eight-week-old pups at the Assistance Dog Institute was being trained for a demonstration. I really wanted the demo to be perfect, so my trainer inadvertently put undue pressure on that puppy. A day before the performance, she called me over to observe. The puppy, who had been retrieving perfectly until that point, turned her head away and walked right past the item she had been successfully picking up for two weeks—as if it didn't even exist! That was a clear sign that she'd had enough. She was fried, and there was nothing we could do about it. Instead of the puppy, I took a videotape to the demo.

Once you've taught your dog the third word, limit her exercises to the first three words for the next several days. Your dog's memory for words, irrespective of how well she seems to know them, is not finely honed. You've both worked hard. Take a nap.

Take a break. If I had to choose between burnout or stopping prematurely, I'd stop prematurely. Reawakening inter-

---

SIGNS OF DOGGIE BURNOUT OR CONFUSION

Until your dog learns to lead you to a flash card that says "Enough is enough," you'll have to watch him for cues that he's had enough education for one day or that he is having problems understanding the word that you are trying to teach him. Stop the reading exercises (remember: always end on a positive note) or help him understand them by giving him hints if he is:

- scratching his collar
- looking away
- easily and obviously distracted by other things in the room
- yawning
- not interested in coming to the area of the room where you usually train him
- lying down and staying put

est after burnout can take weeks to months. Stopping prematurely simply means we are not moving forward quite as fast as we might. But each time I pick up the leash, we are both enthusiastic.

How many exercises are enough? A lot depends on the age of the dog, the time of day, other activities that the dog is engaged in, and the enthusiasm of the dog and the teacher. I find that stopping after three to nine exercises with each new word is almost perfect—for both of us. Here are some general guidelines to help you figure out your dog's limit:

Your dog's personality will also come into play here. If your dog is the serious, analytical type, he may seem to catch on slowly, if only because he is concentrating so hard on getting it right. If he is more of a go-getter with a "driver" personality, he may jump in and offer a response to the flash card too quickly because he is eager to get the exercise over with and get that treat. Again, there are no hard and fast rules about how many exercises are too many for one day. It depends on the dog.

If your dog is	You may do	But . . .
Up to 8 weeks old	3 to 5 exercises with *sit* and *down*	If he is already reading ***down,*** you may introduce ***sit*** and do 3 to 4 more exercises with ***sit***. You may do more exercises with other words if he is reading ***sit*** and ***down*** well. Do just 4 to 5 exercises with each new word.
9 to 12 weeks old	5 to 7 exercises per card	Be careful not to overdo it!
Older than 12 weeks	6 to 9 exercises per card	Don't do any more than 9!

As long as you didn't burn out your dog with too many exercises before you retired your flash cards for the day, tomorrow's exercises will probably go more smoothly. Count on overnight learning to clarify and solidify information in your dog's mind. When you pick up your flash cards after a night's rest, your dog may really focus on the next new word and learn it in only one trial.

ROLL

Part iii

Go: Read, Spot, Read!

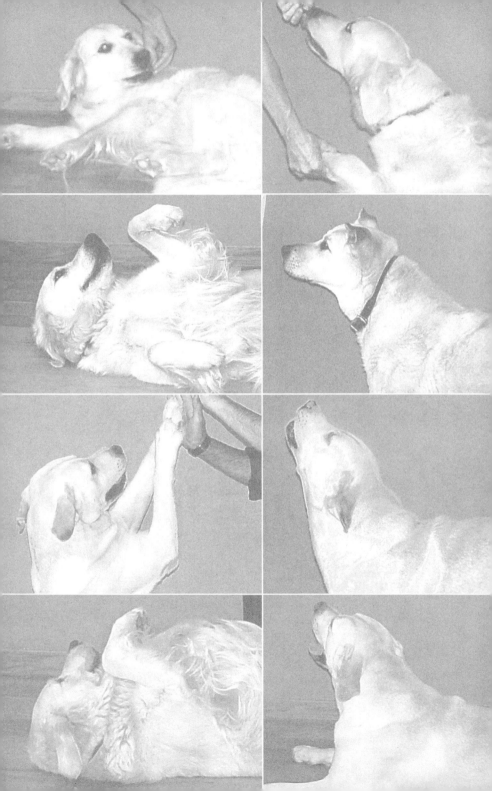

Chapter
5

Teach Your Dog to Read More Words

$\mathcal{C}$hildren learn to read with greater ease if they've grown up in a language-rich environment. Dogs do, too. The more commands your dog knows, the better reader he can be. Once your dog has mastered the basic *sit* and *down* commands, he can advance to more exotic concepts like *stand, roll, turn, shake, speak,* and *bow.* When he can respond to these verbal commands well, he will be ready to respond to their written forms.

Teaching More Basic Commands

$\mathcal{C}$ontinue to channel your excitement carefully as your dog reads more and more. Too much of a good thing can be distracting! I love letting my dog know when he does something right. Almost always, he is a more gung-ho learner due to my exuberance. However, if we are in the middle of a complex training moment and both of us are already fired up to learn, I restrain my enthusiastic expressions (which would just distract us both from the work at hand anyway). A simple "Yes!" immediately followed by a small treat at the conclusion of each exercise will indicate to the dog that he is on the right track. I wait until we successfully reach that training moment's summit to share my pent-up delight with my dog.

Also, remember to pace yourself and your dog as you move from one command to another. Watch for signs of doggie burnout. If you suspect that your dog has reached his limit, wait another day to continue.

Your dog may know only three or four verbal commands; if so, you can teach him to read all of the words in his repertoire by following the steps that you learned in Part II. If your dog knows many commands, I suggest that you teach him to read words in the following order (from easiest to most difficult):

Down: Your dog lowers his entire body to the ground.
Sit: Your dog puts his seat on the ground for a short time.
Stand: Your dog stands up with all four feet on the ground.
Roll: Your dog rolls over and exposes his stomach.
Turn: Your dog turns in a circle.
Shake: Your dog offers his paw in greeting.
Speak: Your dog barks when you tell him to.
Bow: Your dog takes a bow on command.
Up: Your dog puts his front feet on a table edge.
Kiss: Your dog gives you a quick lick on the cheek.
Go to bed: Your dog goes to his special bed or designated sleeping area.

How this command works: When you ask your dog to stand, you want him to get up with all four feet on the ground.

Teaching the verbal command: A dog will stand on his own, but to get him to stand on command, he needs some way to associate the posture with the word *stand*. One simple way to do that is to give the *stand* command when he is sitting or lying down. After you say the word *stand*, take a small step away from him to get him to stand so that he doesn't take a step forward.

Stand is so easy to teach that people seem to need to make it hard. The trick is in the moving away. You have to judge just how much movement it will take on your part to get your dog to stand. Most people retreat too far, and the dog ends up standing and walking forward.

If you do need to take a significant number of steps backward to get your dog to get up, then reverse direction and step *toward* him as he is standing up so that you block his approach. Judge his arousal level. A more excitable dog is more likely to take that extra step or two. A quieter dog is harder to arouse, so you need to convey more enthusiasm to get him to move. You may have to clap your hands or pat your thigh to get your dog to realize that you mean business.

Repeat the word *stand* as he stands up, say "Yes!," and give him a treat. Reaching your hand under his belly and rubbing gently when he does stand will add to the speed at which he will make the association between the posture and the command.

If, while standing, he begins to sink into a sit, move again and he will stand again. By repeating the word *stand* during this exercise, you will help him develop the association.

As with all words, your dog should stand on command (without any movement on your part) before you teach him to read the word *stand*.

Tips for teaching your dog to read the word stand: Your dog should be an adept reader before you introduce the "stand" flash card. Also, unlike most other commands that begin when the dog is in a standing position, your dog should be sitting or lying down before you show him this word.

As you show him this flash card, be careful not to move your shoulders, legs, or hips, or he will just follow your body cues instead of reading the word. You taught him to respond to the verbal command for *stand* by moving your own body, so your body will have a natural tendency to fall into that pattern when you are trying to teach him the written command. Make a concerted effort to stand still.

TEACH YOUR DOG TO READ THE WORD *ROLL*

How this command works: When you ask your dog to roll, she is to turn onto her back with her front and back legs up so that she exposes her stomach to you. This is an important command for service dogs because it allows a person who is physically disabled to visually check the underside of the dog's body for ticks, scratches, and hot spots.

Teaching the verbal command: Give your dog the *down* command. Then gently, while repeating the word *roll*, take a treat and draw it from her nose, across her shoulder, and over her upper back. Position the treat so that her nose will follow it and she will roll onto her back.

Just like the command *sit*, you are using the treat to lure your dog so she moves her head and subsequently her body into the desired posture. If you move the treat too fast or too slowly, or too far from or too close to her nose, she won't fluidly roll into position. So be sure her nose is following the treat! Also, do not take the treat across her neck; instead, make a semicircle around her shoulder. When she first downs, note which haunch she is leaning on (if there is one). Since she is already leaning over slightly on that one side, draw the treat from her nose around her outer shoulder to encourage her to lean more in that direction.

When she rolls, say "Yes!" and give her the treat. Rub her belly as an added incentive to do it next time.

Once your dog rolls readily when you lure her with a treat, while you are standing, hold the treat to the side and make the

same targeting motion with just your finger. When your dog responds readily to this motion, gradually withdraw any targeting cues until your dog responds to the verbal command alone. Give her a treat each time, coupled with enthusiastic praise and belly rubs to help solidify the association.

***Tips for teaching your dog to read the word* roll:** All new teachers of reading tend to try to help the dog do the command by hinting with their body language: a tilt of the head, a roll of the eyes, a slight movement of the body, or a shake of the card. Each of these body language cues actually detracts from your dog's ability to read. If you don't remain perfectly still, she will always look to your movements before focusing on the card because your movements are natural—the card is not. Just as with the *stand* command, when you taught your dog the verbal form of the *roll* command, you had to move your body—in this case to get down and move the treat so your dog could get the idea. When you teach her to read the word *roll,* you shouldn't move at all.

Also, with both the verbal and reading commands for *roll,* make sure there is enough room for your dog to follow through with the motion. If the space is too crowded, your dog will learn to avoid rolling rather than do it with enthusiasm.

TEACH YOUR DOG TO READ THE WORD *TURN*

How this command works: When you ask your dog to turn, you want him to spin in a complete circle in front of you. Dogs, like humans, favor one side or the other, so try both directions to see which one your dog seems to respond to best. Many young and more highly aroused dogs seem to love this command. Maybe it's like being on a roller coaster. Keep it fun with a big smile and an enthusiastic response.

Teaching the verbal command: Entice your dog into a turn by holding a treat in front of his nose while he is facing you. If you move the treat away from him in a circular pattern, he will turn in a circle.

Sometimes trying to draw a big dog into a circular movement is difficult. You need to start with the dog as close to you as possible and lean over to draw the circle. Keep it as tight as you can while accommodating the size of your dog. Dogs can spin in pretty tight circles when they are motivated, so make sure the treat you are luring with is worth it.

When your dog completes the circle, say "Yes!" and reward him with the treat.

After he turns readily, following the treat as a lure, withdraw the treat and target the turn with your finger, fading the cue as he seems to need less help from you. Then treat, praise, and pet enthusiastically!

***Tips for teaching your dog to read the word* turn:** *Turn* is really fun for a dog, but often it is not taught thoroughly. That means that the dog is still relying on a hand signal of some sort. Be sure your dog turns just when you give the verbal command before you teach him to read the word *turn.* And always be sure there is enough room for him to turn!

TEACH YOUR DOG TO READ THE WORD *SHAKE*

How this command works: When you ask your dog to shake, you expect her to offer her paw in greeting.

Teaching the verbal command: If you simply hold out your hand, some dogs will automatically put a paw into it. Other dogs take longer to learn this command. You could spend weeks on this exercise and then one day, for no apparent reason, the dog will respond.

To teach *shake*, start with your dog sitting or standing in front of you. The hardest part of teaching *shake* is that your dog will be inclined to follow your hand movement with her nose, not her paw. So, while repeating the word *shake*, draw her head forward and up toward a treat, just enough so that she will lean forward to get nearer the treat. This forward motion will cause her to barely pick up one leg. Quickly take that leg, say "Yes!" and give her a treat. Don't pull on her leg or paw, or you might pull her off-balance, discouraging her from offering a shake again.

Repeat the same exercise and you will see her becoming more confident with each encounter, lifting her leg farther and farther off the ground until she is clearly handing it to you. Jackpot her efforts with your enthusiasm!

Teach Your Dog to Read More Words

***Tips for teaching your dog to read the word* shake:** In order to
teach your dog to read the word *shake*, she must be able to lift
her paw up on the verbal command *shake*—not just in response to your hand reaching out. To teach her to do this,
gradually delay reaching your hand out when you say
"Shake."

First, hold your hand out to her while you are saying
"Shake." When your dog lifts her paw, say "Yes!" and give
her a treat.

Next, say "Shake" first, followed closely by your hand
reaching out. If she begins to lift her paw before you even

reach your hand out, hooray! Say "Yes!" and take her paw; then give her a treat.

The next time you say "Shake," delay your hand motion a split second longer. Each time she reaches out, say "Yes!" and take her paw, but hold your hand a little higher so she will try to reach up farther.

Don't try to teach her to read *shake* until she is lifting her paw up to her elbow when she hears the command without any hand motion from you at all.

TEACH YOUR DOG TO READ THE WORD *SPEAK*

How this command works: When you ask your dog to speak, you want him to bark on your command.

Pups vocalize to get their mom's attention, so it's always easier to teach *speak* when a dog is young. Later, dogs "speak" to communicate excitement, frustration, threats, pain, or when they want to attract someone's attention. Dogs also bark to express aggression. Thus, more assertive dogs bark easily, whereas it's harder to get a more submissive dog to bark in your face. Almost inevitably, if you are seeking tips to get your dog to speak, you have a more submissive dog. You have to *invite* these dogs to speak, not excite them to speak. They don't want to be aggressive with you.

Tune in to your dog's personality. Instead of using one blanket method to teach him this command, consider what makes him tick when you invite him to speak. What does it take to get him to vocalize? Whatever it is, try to replicate it, or try one of the following methods.

Teaching the verbal command: The point of teaching your dog to speak is to get him to bark when you want him to. To accomplish that, his bark has to be really learned, not just a result of momentary excitement.

All dogs can learn to bark on command. If they know you'll listen, they'll be more likely to communicate. As with every other aspect of dog training, trust and communication between you and your dog help significantly.

Use your dog's natural desire to stay in sync with you physically and emotionally to teach him this command. If you jump up and down, run in place, dance and sing like Elvis ("You ain't nothin' but a hound dog"), show him that you're fired up, and make a variety of upbeat, strange, and fascinating noises, you can raise your dog's excitement to a pitch that probably will result in an enthusiastic bark.

You can place a less assertive or reluctant dog alone inside a fenced-in area with you on the other side of the fence. Do not get too close to the fence. A distance of about three feet between you and your dog makes you seem less overbearing and allows him to feel less uncomfortable about barking at you.

First, let your dog explore the enclosed area. When he is finished, he will come up to the fence to visit with you. Bend over slightly at the waist, look excited, gather your four fingers behind your thumb, then flick them forward quickly and in a whisper-soft suspenseful voice, say "Speak!" As you engage your dog in this play, get him pumped up enough to jump on the fence or simply look enthusiastic. If you see even a tiny indication of arousal, say "Yes!" and give him a treat.

Repeat your playful provocation, whispering "Speak!" again and again. As your dog's response escalates bit by bit, you are building his likelihood to bark, so keep up the anticipation. Fence fighting is such fun for dogs!

Mellower dogs will speak, but teaching them to do so

could take weeks of exercises. If your dog is timid or extremely laid back, as you put him on the other side of a fence, you will need to invite, encourage, and let him know it's okay to talk to you — in fact, it's what you want! You have to mark his every little puff of breath, every little mouth opening, every little pawing of the fence, or any indication he is trying to tell you with his body language that he wants to get to the other side of the fence to be with you. When he begins to see you are listening, he will try harder, which will inevitably lead to a bark.

Another method that might work with your dog is to crate him. Then walk just out of sight and make noises that will cause him to be frustrated enough at his isolation to bark. You also might call him, throw a ball, run, play with another dog, or do something that will provoke him enough to protest.

If you have another dog who does bark on command, get

him to set the example. Reward his efforts in front of the trainee (the dog who is learning to speak) until the trainee decides to join in.

If your dog is not very talkative, wait until he is in a situation in which he barks naturally—for instance, when the mail carrier comes to the door. As soon as you think he will begin to bark, say "Speak!" With enough reinforcement, eventually he will bark at your command.

Another technique is to blow high notes on a harmonica until you get some corresponding vocals from your dog. My husband, Jim, takes his dog Nugget out on stage at his barbecue restaurant, and they sing the blues together.

No matter what you do to elicit a bark from your dog, as soon as he speaks on command, reward him with a "Yes!" and a treat.

***Tips for teaching your dog to read the word* speak:** Your dog can speak from either a standing or a sitting position.

Speak is an easy command for you to facilitate with your body language and facial expressions, so be careful not to give your dog any hints. You want him to read the command from the card alone.

Also, while dogs are learning to read, they often vocalize. We let them get away with this at the beginning because their sounds express their frustration and excitement about this new exercise. If your dog is a talker, you can use his natural inclination to comment while you're teaching him to read the word *speak*. To help him make the association between his barks and the "speak" flash card, mark his barks just after he has looked at the card with a well-placed, timely, and enthusiastic "Yes!"

How this command works: When you ask your dog to bow, you want her to lean forward on command, putting the elbows of her front legs on the ground while her butt is up in the air.

Teaching the verbal command: A young or energetic dog often will do what is called a play bow—a solicitation to another dog (or person) to frolic with her. Since she uses this posture to ask you to play, hype up your energy and get playful.

The ideal teaching opportunity for this command is when your dog is already revved up to do it on her own. No one knows your dog better than you. If you are aware of when your dog is about to make this motion, say "Bow" just before she actually does it. Be careful not to be so exuberant that you distract her from completing the bow by inadvertently redirecting her attention to you. Follow her accurate response to the word *bow* with a "Yes!" and a treat. Although she'll learn best if you say the command right before she

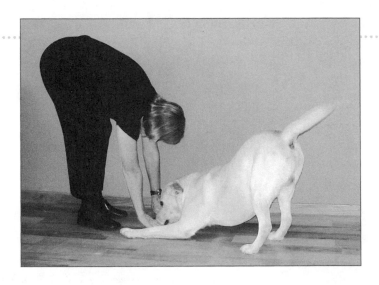

bows, if she's a fast learner, you won't undercut her ability to learn the command even if you come in a bit late with the word *bow*.

Another approach, which again is best when your dog is in a playful mood, is to bend over while saying "Bow." Your dog may try to copy your movements and may bow herself. If she starts to down, take a step back so that she stands, and repeat the bow motion. Again, that "Yes!" and treat are critical.

A third way to teach this command starts with your dog standing in front of you. Reach down to the floor with a treat in your hand as you say "Bow." You are attempting to lure her into following your hand with her head. Some dogs will go into a complete down posture immediately; others will lower only the front part of their bodies.

If your dog does bow, get that "Yes!" out immediately to let her know that she has gotten herself into the posture you are seeking. If, in the beginning, you are getting only a partial response (just her head going to your hand), reinforce her effort anyway. Partial responses mean your dog is moving forward bit by bit, which is how learning takes place. if her back end repeatedly downs when her front does, stand perpendicular to her body. Lure her head to the floor with a treat in your weakest hand (if you are right-handed your weakest hand is your left, and vice versa). Use your strongest hand to touch her underbelly to discourage her rear from sinking to the ground. Repeat the exercise with a timely "Yes!" to let your dog know that you want a bow, not a down.

Tips for teaching your dog to read the word bow: A playful dog loves to bow; a more serious dog doesn't. And, just as with the other commands, your dog must respond well to the verbal command before you ask her to read the word *bow*.

When you are teaching your dog to read this command, your head will bob naturally if you are not very careful. Remember that reading is about looking at the words, not taking cues from body language. Stand still. However, since bow is a playful command, feel free to put a smile on your face!

TEACH YOUR DOG TO READ THE WORD *UP*

How this command works: When you give your dog the *up* command, you want him to put his front paws up on a surface that you have indicated (such as a bed, table, countertop, wall, or garbage can). This is a useful command for service dogs who "up" to give money to store clerks and to reach light switches and telephones. Some people like their dogs to up so they can rub their bellies. That's fine—but don't

let your dog up on the kitchen table or anywhere else where there is food.

Teaching the verbal command: Start by teaching your dog the *up* command on a table or other surface with an edge so that he can balance himself.

As the two of you draw near to the table, quickly reach your arm out and target the table edge. Tap it while repeating the word *up*. The position of your hand will make it awkward for your dog's paws to move beyond it; this will reduce his incentive to try to jump all the way up on the table. However, a more enthusiastic dog may not be deterred, so be ready to stop his eager flight!

You may need to generate a lot of enthusiasm and verbal encouragement to get a calmer dog to put his front paws on the table edge the first time. You may even need to pick up his front legs gently and place them there just so he knows it's okay with you. To encourage his future efforts, an enthusiastic "Yes!" and treat should reward this accomplishment.

Once your dog is experienced with following the *up* command on a table edge, you can teach him to up on a wall. Be aware, though, that this movement requires even more balance than upping on something with an edge.

Tap the wall slightly below where his head would be in that up position. When he ups, do not expect him to remain there! Say "Yes!" immediately so he can get down. Then, each time you ask him to up, delay the "Yes!" slightly so he will remain there longer. If you don't overdo it, he will lengthen the time he stays in that posture waiting for your "Yes!" before coming back down. Eventually his balance will improve such that he will be able to hold that position long enough to turn a light switch on or off without slipping.

***Tips for teaching your dog to read the word* up:** When you use a prop like a table or a wall for the first time, stand beside it so that your dog does not have to turn away from you in order to follow through on the command. Later, in increments, you can change your position so that your dog has to turn from you and walk all the way across the room to carry out the command. Initially, though, make it as easy as possible for him to understand without letting the prop cue him to the

command. Instead, while standing beside the table, show him two or three other words first. A *down* and *sit* command before you ask for an *up* would be a good diversion. Then give the *up* command. If he knows the word well, he will look at you, look at the table, look at you, and up on the table's edge.

TEACH YOUR DOG TO READ THE WORD *KISS*

How this command works: When you ask your dog for a kiss, you want her to give you a quick dart of her tongue on your cheek. When done right, this is a sweet interaction.

Teaching the verbal command: Most people assume that leaning toward a dog invites her kiss. This is not true of people or dogs! Rather, something moving toward you automatically causes you to move away. Until your dog knows the *kiss* command, don't move toward her head. Entice her to move her head toward yours.

Usually if you purse your lips and make kissy noises interspersed with the *kiss* word, your dog will have enough incentive to give you a kiss. If not, you can put some sticky foodstuff, like peanut butter, on your cheek, then present that cheek and the word *kiss* to your dog for her response.

My husband also discovered a reflex method. If you pinch your dog's nostrils together for a few seconds and then release them, her tongue will protrude briefly. If you can get your cheek in the way while saying "Kiss," you can help your

dog develop an association between putting her tongue on your cheek and the word *kiss*.

Tips for teaching your dog to read the word **kiss:** Although your dog should be standing in front of you for most reading commands, it's easier for your dog to give you a kiss if you are sitting on the floor next to her or sitting in a chair with her front legs on your lap, or if her front paws are up on a small table with you on the opposite side so that your face is within her reach.

When you show the "kiss" flash card, it will be up to your dog to figure out a way to give you that kiss. Don't ask for a kiss unless you are in a physically available position, or she will feel like a loser.

One of my staff members allows her dog to up on her chest and give her a kiss, but most people don't want their dogs to jump on them. It's up to you!

TEACH YOUR DOG TO READ THE PHRASE *GO TO BED*

How this command works: When you give your dog the *go to bed* command, you want him to go to his special bed or designated sleeping area and lie down.

This is a pretty sophisticated command. Your dog needs to understand the name for the item "bed." He also needs to know what a bed is for—he is supposed to lie down on it (not too difficult to learn if it is comfy). Last, when you say the phrase *go to* coupled with *bed*, he is to walk over to his bed and lie down.

You thus teach this command in three stages:

1. First you name the object (*bed*).
2. Then you show him what to do on that object (lie *down*).
3. Finally you teach him to *go* to it when you tell him.

If you have more than one dog bed available, your dog will need to choose one, and that could confuse him, especially during the early stages of his learning. Make things as simple as possible, and put all but one bed away.

Ultimately, you want to concentrate on giving the command *go to bed* without needing to say "Down" or to finger-point. If you still need to point to the bed or walk your dog to the bed, teaching him to read *go to bed* will be difficult.

Teaching the verbal command: Link this command to other words that your dog already knows. If you can help him to transfer his older knowledge of the command *down* into a newer context, you will speed up his learning time considerably.

Start by taking your dog to his bed and repeating the word *bed* while patting it. Your dog probably will try to follow your targeting by stepping onto the bed. Go ahead and encourage that by saying "Yes!" and give him a treat. Then

quickly continue: "Bed, bed, down." When your dog downs, say "Yes!" and give him another treat.

Next, call your dog off the bed and repeat the exercise. When he moves onto the bed and readily downs, change from patting the bed to pointing to the bed. Once you can eliminate the word *down* and need only to point and say "Bed" in order for your dog to lie down, you may move to the next step.

So far you have helped your dog make an association between his bed and the word *bed* and between the word *bed* and the concept of downing right there. At this point, don't be concerned if your dog doesn't put his entire body on the bed. Accept less than perfection at first, and then refine.

Now call your dog and together walk a few feet away from his bed. Then turn and approach the bed again. Try to stay slightly ahead of him so that you are better situated to

sweep your arm toward the bed and pat it, if necessary, while repeating "Bed, go to bed." If your dog goes to the bed but just stands on it, say "Down" to get your point across.

Continue to repeat this exercise. As your dog comfortably downs when you give the *go to bed* command, strengthen the *go* command by encouraging him to walk slightly in front of you as the two of you approach the bed. Bend over and hold your arm so that you can point your finger out in front of your dog as you approach the bed. Next, point, but walk behind your dog, until finally you can simply point and he will walk ahead of you, go directly to his bed, and lie down. Voilà!

Tips for teaching your dog to read the phrase go to bed: This command requires the dog to move from one location to another, so start close to the bed when you hold up the flash card while saying "Go to bed." Then increase the distance, just as you did when teaching him the verbal command.

Your dog is learning shapes of letters as abstract concepts, so the leap to three words (*go to bed*) is not difficult; in fact, it may be easier for him to read this command because it is distinctly different from the other words he has learned. When, at a much more sophisticated level of reading, a flash card tells your dog to "get the shoe," he will have to learn to discriminate between the shapes of the letters more carefully.

More than a Kiss and a Shake

*I*f your dog is swiftly offering you a smooch or a shake when she sees those words on flash cards, she gets it! Keep adding to the words in her memory bank by trying other commands that she already knows. If she's familiar with the verbal or hand motion command, she should be able to read its written form just by following the same steps you have used to teach her to read other words. There's no limit to the commands your dog can read!

Why teach her more words? The more comfortable she is with reading words on flash cards, the easier it will be for her to bound ahead to the next stage of her reading progress — reading stick figures and symbols.

Chapter
6

Teach Your Dog to Respond to Stick Figures and Symbols

*T*he year 2003 was truly a "leap" year at the Assistance Dog Institute, because that was when we made the astounding jump from teaching dogs basic commands, such as *retrieve* and *heel,* to teaching them to read! In the first part of that year, I taught more and more dogs to read, and I learned more and more about showing people how to teach them.

The fact that dogs could read held such fascination for me that I spent a good part of that summer researching human reading. What I found blew me away! First, humans are *not* prewired to read; as parents, teachers, and children themselves know, people have to work hard to learn this skill. For some reason, knowing this made it less, rather than more, surprising that dogs could read, too. Like people, they just need to be taught.

I also discovered that humans first began to read somewhat detailed pictures. They later moved to stick figures and then to words. Serendipitously, my dogs learned to read written words first simply because that was the experiment we began with. Their success got me thinking about the evolution of reading in humans, though, and the more I read about the subject, the more I was inspired to see how dogs would respond to pictures.

How My Own Dogs Learned to Read Stick Figures

*a*t first I pulled out photographs of dogs in different postures (like sitting and downing) and showed them to my dogs. Their lackluster reactions disappointed me. Keila, my brilliant black Lab, did ape the dogs in the photographs nicely, and Nexus, my savvy white golden retriever, responded even better. Even so, after the thrill of teaching them to read written words, this type of reading just didn't grab me.

To make things more interesting, instead of photographs, I tried computer-generated stick figures of dogs. I modeled these figures after a metal plant stand in the shape of a dog that my husband surprised me with a couple of birthdays ago. Unlike the pale photos, these images of black shapes on white paper were rich with contrast. I used one head and body shape for all of the figures and manipulated these shapes into different postures so that one figure was sitting, one figure was downing, and so forth.

SIT

As I got ready to show these cartoonish images to my dogs, I decided to reverse the order in which I would present the cards. Instead of starting with *down*, I would start with *sit* so that I could head off the dogs' expectation that every pattern of flash-card lessons begins with *down*.

I showed the first card, "sit," to Nexus, and I went through the same steps I had used when I taught her to read words. I showed the flash card to her three times with the spoken word and then presented the card without the spoken word. Not surprisingly, she sat each and every time.

DOWN

Next I went through the same teaching exercise with the "down" stick-figure card. Nexus looked at the card, and she downed every time. No problem!

ROLL

Then I showed her the "roll" card, but I didn't have time to cue her with the spoken word because something in another part of the room caught my attention. When I turned back, she was rolling! I was shocked. I had assumed that I would have to teach each of the stick figures just as I had taught each of the written words. It never dawned on me that a dog could learn the postures of the first two stick figures, then apply that concept to other stick-figure postures, responding to them without any cues from me.

TURN

Astonished and elated with the results of this experiment, I went back to my computer and made another stick figure. This time I used the same stick-figure dog doing a turn. At the institute, we teach very young dogs to turn by spinning all the way around in a circle. Later we use that same command for half-turns. That way, when a person with a disability is grooming them, they will readily present whichever side of the body the person needs to brush. (Also, the dogs often wear a backpack, so the turn command allows the person to access both sides of it.)

The "turn" stick figure that I created looked bizarre to me. It was basically the body of a dog going one way and the head going the other. I couldn't imagine how Nexus could possibly understand that it meant *turn*.

She looked at the card twice and then she rolled and sat—she was offering other behaviors in the hopes of responding

accurately to the card. As I've mentioned, sometimes reading dogs will respond with unexpected behaviors, perhaps in a quest for treats. They hope if they go through their repertoire of movements, eventually they'll find one that will lead to the prize. You can tell if they are really reading by the percentage of accurate first responses they make.

Finally, Nexus quietly stared at the flash card and turned. This was unbelievable. She had not offered a turn before, so I knew she wasn't throwing "turn" into the mix out of desperation. I was astounded. She was looking at the flash card and figuring out what it was about!

UP

Once Nexus did a roll and a turn, I was on a roll, too! I took the same stick-figure image of the dog and manipulated it on the computer so that its front paws were up on a tabletop. Then I took Nexus to one of my college classes. I told the students I was going to try a new card that she had seen only once before. I stood fairly near a tabletop, but not one that she had ever upped on before.

After I called Nexus over to me, I gave her a treat. She was excited and paying attention—just the right balance for learning something new. I gave her another treat, then showed her the "sit" stick figure. She sat. Next, I showed her the "down" stick figure. She literally threw herself to the

ground. Then I brought out the "up" stick figure card from behind my back and showed it to her, holding it in the same position as I held the other two cards.

Nexus looked at the card, looked at me, looked at the card again, looked at the table, and then she upped on the table beside me! At that point for me, it was a given: Dogs can read, not just by simple associative learning, but with real thinking, deductive reasoning, and comprehension!

A Stick-Figure Epiphany

*E*ven as my own dogs began to read stick figures, I tried to learn more about the evolution of early human reading. One day I found a book that included a photograph of a funny sign in New Mexico that was thousands of years old. In this photograph, a stick figure of a man on a horse upside-down, their feet in the air, warned that it would be dangerous for a horse and rider to set off into the mountains. Beside this image, a figure of an upright mountain goat suggested that it *would* be safe for a mountain goat to proceed.

It struck me that this sign was very similar to the "roll" stick figure I had created on my computer for my dogs. I'm awed by the fact that in just the last few years, they have picked up the meanings of both stick figures and written words—an array of symbols that took humans several millennia to wrap their minds around. How much further can they go?

In time, dogs may be able to read and understand a series of symbols like those etched in the mountainside in Arizona. More powerfully, they may someday "speak" to us with a similar message of warning by pointing to cards with words or symbols that they have learned. Once again their increasing knowledge can open doors, not just so we can communicate better with them, but so they can communicate back with us.

How Your Dog Can Read Stick Figures

Once your dog can respond well to verbal commands and can read some written words, she can move on to reading stick figures. (Flash cards of words and stick figures can be downloaded from www.assistancedog.org/readingdogs.) Most dogs—like my wonder dog, Nexus—can spontaneously take their cues from these images of dogs in different postures (for example, sitting, standing, turning). They don't need any verbal prompting to show them what to do. Others may need a little more help. Either way, they must be good at reading words from flash cards first so they know that a flash card, a static piece of paper, has a message just for them.

Your dog, like Nexus, may be a whiz at imitating cartoonish dogs on flash cards. You may be stunned by your superfluous role in silently holding up a card that she automatically responds to! If she is adept at responding to verbal commands and flash-card word commands, she may well be able to respond to the stick figure of a dog in the corresponding position *with no training at all.* That's the wonder of it — the dog figures it out!

If your dog doesn't catch on right away, don't lose heart. You may simply need to strengthen her word reading a little more.

If she is ready to move on to stick-figure reading, but she doesn't seem to be responding to these cards without a verbal hint, go ahead and teach her. You are familiar with the method by now: Show her the card, say the word, give her a chance to do the behavior, say "Yes!," reward her with a treat, and praise her. Do this exercise three times. Then see if she can figure it out without your verbal assist.

If you're uncertain about how to navigate your way through this area, read through the following suggestions for teaching your dog to respond accurately to stick-figure symbols.

The First Stick-Figure Word: Sit

*B*efore you try this exercise, make sure your dog can readily and easily respond to both the verbal command *sit* and the word *sit* on a flash card without prompting. He will be more apt to decipher stick figures without your help if he is very solid with word reading — that is, if he knows exactly what a flash card is for. ("Solid" implies he has been reading words successfully for several days at least and that he is getting most words correct on the first trial.)

Now grab a handful of treats and your laminated stick-figure flash card of a sitting dog.

Make sure both you and your dog are in the right mood for school. Once again, every dog is different. Some dogs will respond better to stick-figure reading after they've had a warm-up of word reading. Others have a shorter attention span; for these dogs, it's better to start cold with stick figures and get right into it.

Your job as a trainer is to set the pace for your dog's learning. Remember not to rush ahead too quickly, or your dog will become confused and you may exhaust his patience. Follow the steps below, and go slowly. I will walk you through two sets of instructions: The first affords your dog the opportunity to figure out stick figures on his own; the second shows you how to teach him to respond to stick figures if he doesn't catch on by himself.

Give Your Dog a Chance to Read Stick Figures on His Own: The Skip-a-Step Lesson

This exercise gives your dog a chance to use his fantastic mind to make sense of a stick figure on his own, without any verbal prompting from you.

Step 1. All Paws on Deck

Call your dog so that he is standing before you, ready to learn.

Step 2. Present the Card

Ta-da! Hold a treat in one hand, or put it on a table nearby. Draw the flash card from behind your back and show it to your dog. Make sure the card is right-side up and hold it very still. Glance down at the card; do not make eye contact with your dog.

Step 3. Skip This Step; Do Not Say the Word Sit

Step 4. Hold It

Don't jiggle the card around. Give your dog a chance to figure it out. Don't take this opportunity away from him unless it's clear that he isn't getting it.

If you can tell that he's about to get discouraged, encourage him with "What's it say?" The more solidly he learned to read the word *sit*, the more likely it is that he will get the stick figure.

If he is still downing as soon as he sits, catch the sit with a "Yes!" before he goes into a down.

With a stick-figure concept as easy as "sit," don't keep going after seven to nine attempts if your dog isn't catching on. If he still doesn't have a clue (or he appears to be getting discouraged despite your "What's it say?"), gently say the word to save him from defeat. Just be sure that he really needs your hint.

Step 5. Bestow Booty and Praise

As soon as your dog sits, say "Yes!" Then give him a treat, pet him, and praise him with gusto.

Once your dog does it right, don't keep repeating the same exercise over and over again with each stick-figure concept. This is a cognitive figuring-it-out exercise rather than an association-building one. Go through the five steps (Step 3 being "do not say the word") a couple more times with your dog. Then move on to the next stick figure.

Teach Your Dog to Read Stick Figures: The Five-Step Lesson

*I*f your dog had trouble with the previous exercise, relax! Try the exercise again, but do not skip Step 3. Use the verbal prompt until he gets his signs straight.

Then let him try the stick figure, but don't say the word.

The Second Stick-Figure Word: <u>Down</u>

*J*ust as with the "sit" flash card, make sure that your dog can respond to both the verbal and written forms of *down* before you introduce the stick-figure card. Proceed with the "down" card. Only say the word "down" if your dog has not figured it out for herself.

When your dog responds to both the "sit" and "down" stick-figure cards with aplomb, you can mix up the cards to see if she is really reading these images. Try two sits followed by one down with treats, petting, and praise at the end. Then try two downs and one sit with the same sequence of rewards at the end.

When you mix up the cards, limit your exercises to two or three sessions of a series of three to five cards per day. Don't do more, or you may burn your dog out. Even if she knows the stick figures, she may refuse to respond.

As you add more cards to your dog's repertoire, increase the length of each session very slowly. You must take into account that the more words she learns, the more stressed she will be to remember. You don't want her to fail because she's dog tired and you're pushing too much. If you aren't in any hurry, she will have that much more time for overnight learning. In time, the words will settle into her mind and she'll be reading like a champ.

Build Your Dog's Stick-Figure Repertoire

*A*fter you and your dog have had a good night's sleep, try another one or two easy stick figures to see if your dog can figure them out for himself without any verbal hints from you. (Again, he should know both the verbal commands and the written words well first.) I usually suggest that people move on with discrete commands (such as *roll, up, bow, turn,* and *shake*) that a dog can perform from start to finish with no extra movement on the part of the trainer.

If you've had to teach your dog to read the "sit" and "down" stick figures by saying the words, and you've been carefully walking him through the five steps each time, *now is the time to* not *say the word and let him try to figure it out on his own.*

TEACH YOUR DOG TO READ THE STICK FIGURE FOR *SHAKE*

How this command works: Dogs pick up on patterns and movements, and they quickly take in the outlines of objects that they see, but they are not famous for noticing details. I once took a dog named Buddy along when I was traveling to a conference in Orlando, Florida. Kent, a seminar student who had worked with Buddy for a couple weeks about six months before, was also coming to the conference and was looking forward to seeing Buddy.

Kent drove up curbside in a convertible as Buddy and I were standing on the sidewalk outside the conference center.

As we walked toward the car, I expected Buddy to recognize Kent at any minute. But dogs aren't oriented to particular facial features, especially from a distance. Buddy showed no recognition whatsoever. Even as I began to speak with Kent, the dog did not respond to his voice. He just stood quietly and politely beside me as Kent and I talked. Kent remained sitting in the convertible.

Suddenly Buddy's head went down to the ground and then up again as he took a huge sniff. An enormous smile spread across his face and then he leaped four feet in the air, over the car door, and right into Kent's lap. Buddy's sense of smell had trumped every other form of perception!

My experience with dogs like Buddy kept some of my enthusiasm in check as I made more stick figures for my dogs, especially because some of these figures had more subtle features. For instance, when I first made a flash card for the word *shake*, I used the graphics program on my computer to lift one of the two legs of the "sit" dog figure into the shake position. Knowing what I do about a dog's attention to detail, I had grave reservations about whether any of the dogs who were trying these exercises would really notice that the dog in the picture had a leg up.

After I printed the "shake" card, I handed it to one of my staff members, a very detail-oriented person who does all of our accounting. I asked her to laminate the card and then write the name of the command on the back so we would have a cue to hold the card upright.

She laminated the card for me and returned it. When I turned it over, I saw that she had written the word *sit* in the upper corner. Even *she* didn't notice that I had changed the card by lifting one of the dog's paws up in a shake position, so of course I wondered how a dog would ever pick up on this minor detail.

I first tried this card out with Norton, my colleague Jorjan's dog. He knows many verbal commands, including shake, and he is also a great reader. I handed the card to Jorjan and she showed it to Norton. During his reading lessons, Norton sometimes offers a few behaviors (such as sit and down) when he is trying to figure out what a flash card says, but he had never offered a shake before.

As Jorjan held the card, Norton looked at it, touched it with his nose, sniffed it, sat, downed, got back up, downed, and rolled. Then he got back up again and looked at the card for several seconds. We could tell that he was really concentrating. Then suddenly he tentatively lifted his paw three or four inches off the ground! We were elated! Dogs *do* notice subtle changes in images after all, especially when they are truly focusing.

Jorjan showed Norton the card again and, with more confidence this time, he lifted his paw even higher.

A few days later, a client of ours whom I mentioned earlier, Steve Sweeney, came to visit with his current service dog, Quest. Steve's speech is very hard to understand. When I first met him, I couldn't understand a thing he said. When he started interacting with our service dogs, he had to work on his speech so they could understand him. Steve has made remarkable improvement as he has learned to communicate with the three service dogs who have worked with him over the years.

Quest is a sweet and devoted being with an average level of energy. When Steve came into the room in his wheelchair with her, I handed him the "shake" card and I asked him to just hold it for her without saying anything. Although Quest had seen a few flash cards with stick figures, her repertoire with them was limited.

Because of his disability, Steve isn't able to hold objects

completely still, but nevertheless he took the flash card and held it. Quest played around, took a sideways glance at it, and played around some more. When a dog doesn't make an effort to read a command, we just say the word "No." When Steve said "No" to Quest, she stopped goofing off and focused on the card. Then, just like Norton, she slowly raised her paw a few inches off the ground. It was an amazing moment for all of us!

Next I asked a graduate of ours named Alex to try the "shake" stick-figure card with her dog. Alex is continuing her postgraduate education at a local college and working for us part time. Just prior to her college graduation, she asked to adopt one of our social therapy dogs, Xiana, a yellow Lab. Now Alex devotes much of her free time to volunteer work with Xiana in hospitals, schools, and most recently in our crisis response team program, sharing Xiana's unconditional love with children who have been separated from their parents due to a family crisis of one sort or another. They are a fabulous team, committed to each other and to doing good.

First, I made sure (as I had with Norton and Quest) that Xiana knew how to lift her paw to the verbal command *shake* without Alex having to cue her by reaching out to take it. She knew how to do this. I also verified that she had been taught to read. Like all of the dogs at the institute, she had been taught to read words, but Xiana had never seen stick-figure flash cards before, so this exercise was brand new. When Alex showed her the card, Xiana responded just like Norton and Quest: She looked at the card, concentrated, and slowly lifted her paw.

Just last month I experimented with a younger dog who was just beginning to learn to read. Kelly, one of our very able college students, was nearing graduation and wanted to include more reading in her dog Frank's repertoire. Frank, a beautiful golden retriever puppy, had been with Kelly for seven months, and they had a strong bond.

Kelly tested Frank's ability to lift his paw to the verbal command *shake* without a physical cue. He did. Nevertheless, Frank had minimal reading under his belt and had seen no stick figures at all, so we set our expectations low.

First, Kelly showed him the stick figure for *sit,* and he sat. Then she showed him the stick figure for "down," and he downed. When Kelly pulled out the stick figure for *shake,* Frank went through just about every command he had been taught, without offering a shake. Kelly's "What's it say?" encouraged him and kept up his enthusiasm to try.

Then, surprising us all, he lifted his front paws one at a time, like a prancing horse. Even Frank, with less experience to go on, made some connection with the leg-up posture of the stick figure. A more solid foundation of reading undoubtedly would have helped him get it right sooner and more accurately. But he did recognize the position of the stick figure, and he did come close to imitating what he saw. Talk about bit-by-bit learning!

***Tips for teaching your dog to read the stick figure for* shake:** All of the dogs whom we have trained to read the stick figure for *shake* knew the verbal command for *shake* well ahead of time. They also knew that "Shake" means they should lift a paw without a human partner providing a physical cue by stooping down to hold it (see p. 100).

When your dog is proficient in lifting his paw to the verbal command and is reading the word *shake,* try the stick figure for *shake.* If he makes any movement that shows he is figuring out what that stick figure means, say "Yes!" and give him copious treats and positive feedback. Bit by bit, his ability to shake will improve when he sees the stick figure of a dog doing the same.

TEACH YOUR DOG TO READ THE STICK FIGURE FOR *TURN*

Turning in response to the "turn" stick figure is easy for some dogs and tough for others. This is definitely not a slam-dunk stick figure. Most of my human staff members were not able

to figure it out. If your dog doesn't do it within the first four or five tries, but is very good at reading the written word *turn*, revisit the steps you used to teach the written word (see p. 96). Give the smallest cue necessary to help your dog understand what the stick figure is meant to represent.

Japanese and Chinese Characters

*I*n May 2003 I was invited to Japan to teach sixty students in a dog training workshop. I asked my hosts to help me make flash cards with the Japanese translations of words (*sit, down, stand,* and *roll*) that we had taught our dogs to read in English. Because Japanese characters seem complicated to me, with their many and varied strokes, I doubted that a dog could learn or memorize them. Nevertheless, I took flash cards with both English letters and Japanese characters to class.

Just as with English words, we chose Japanese words in which the first and last characters were distinctly different from each of the other words we were teaching. I guided the students through the exercises, and much to my shock, the dogs who were exposed to the Japanese characters were as quick to learn and respond as the ones who were exposed to the English letters. So far the only limit to a dog's ability to learn appears to be our unwillingness or lack of opportunity to try!

In May 2005 I again taught a weeklong seminar in Japan. During the first four days, I gave lectures about canine educational psychology interspersed with practical sessions that covered lots of commands, including teaching dogs to tug open and shut doors, pick up dropped items, and turn on light switches. I also explained how to teach dogs to read the words *sit, down, roll, stand, shake, bow,* and *turn*.

On the fifth day, I had each of the twenty dogs in the class come to the front to read stick figures that corresponded to the written words they had just been taught to read. I had no idea what would happen because the opportunity to practice reading words had been so limited. Every single dog was able to do it—some read more stick figures than others, some hesitantly, but they all read at least one word! It was a remarkable response in such a short time. This experience also confirmed my suspicion that the dogs who are most experienced at reading words in turn become the most accurate stick-figure readers.

Other Symbols

When your dog is reading some of these basic stick figures, you can try additional ones, such as *up, roll, bow,*

and *stand*. Recently I added to my dogs' stick-figure reper-
toires with new figures showing a dog with his mouth open
(for "speak"); a dog sticking out his tongue (for "kiss"); and
a dog on a bed (for "go to bed"). I tested these stick-figure
symbols on our expert reader, Norton. Success again! I have
yet to find the limit to a dog's mind! (You can download
these symbols from our website: www.assistancedog.org/
readingdogs.)

TEACH YOUR DOG TO HONOR THE "⊘" SYMBOL

A dog can learn the quasi-universal symbol for "No," "Don't
go there," or "Leave it alone." Taught later in life, an older,
less sensitive dog may not be trusted to follow the directive
without you present. Taught young, a sensitive dog might
honor it even if it's in front of a delicious steak and you are
gone for hours. At least it's worth a try. But first you must
teach the *leave it* command.

1. **Rig a temptation.** With your dog sitting in front of you,
   and watching, hold a food treat in your hand near his
   nose.
2. **Give him a verbal warning.** As soon as your dog shows interest in the treat, tell him "no" or "leave it!" Be as emphatic as
   necessary to get your point across. An object in motion
   tends to stay in motion, so stopping your dog before he
   moves toward the treat, when he is just thinking about it, is
   the best strategy. (If he ignores your order and moves
   toward the treat, give him a gentle bump on the nose with
   your hand.)
3. **Teach him the *release* command.** After a very short wait,
   with your dog responding to your command, say "Release." Say it in an upbeat voice that makes it clear he can

have the treat you are holding. Do this exercise several times. Lengthen the time he has to "leave it" before giving the *release* command little by little. When he is showing solid self-restraint, move to the next step.

4. **Teach him the "⊘" symbol.** When your dog knows the verbal *leave it* command soundly, once again hold a treat near his nose, but this time insert a flash card of the "⊘" symbol in a plastic picture frame between his nose and the treat when you give the *leave it* command. After a short time, remove the flash card and say "Release."

5. **Strengthen his response to the "⊘" symbol.** Again hold the flash card between a treat and your dog's nose. This time remove the card, but refrain from saying, "Release." When your dog looks at you to see if this means he can take the treat smile encouragingly. You may even need to move the treat toward him to help him get the idea that the removal of the card is the equivalent of "Release." Do this exercise several times before moving on to the next step.

6. **Halo or horns.** This step requires the utmost care. You now want to allow your dog more latitude regarding the "leave it" symbol. However, if he gets the treat, all bets are off and you will need to start from scratch. Hold the treat near your dog's nose while you simultaneously place the picture frame with the flash card of the "⊘" symbol in front of the treat. Do not say anything. If your dog has come to understand the role of the symbol, he will look at it, look at you, look at it, and wait. Now remove the symbol to allow him to gain access to the treat! Yes! Repeat this step in different places so that he learns to respect it.

7. **Reward his restraint with more challenges.** For safety's sake, you might want to put the treat in a Kong so that if your dog gets by you, he won't be able to wolf down the treat and thus lose all respect for the "⊘" symbol that you

have been so carefully building. With your dog beside you, put the treat (in the Kong) on the ground or a chair seat. At the same time, place the picture frame of the "⊘" symbol in front of the treat. This is a new context, so your dog may try to sniff around the picture frame. If he does, remind him in no uncertain terms to "leave it." When your dog ignores the treat for a short while, once again remove the "⊘" symbol and let your dog have the treat.

Enhance your exercise by leaving the "⊘" symbol close to the Kong as you gradually move farther and farther away from it. Continue to give the *release* command when you remove the symbol. Never leave the symbol within your dog's sight after you give the *release* command, or it will lose its meaning. Over time, stop using verbal cues and continue to reward your dog for his self-control.

8. Lay down the law. Now use the "⊘" symbol in other areas that you want to define as out of bounds: a chair that your dog is not allowed to sleep on, food on the kitchen table, a room you do not want him to enter, an area of the yard that is off-limits, a plant he is not to nose, a bird cage he should keep his distance from, and so on. For each area, teach your dog the verbal "Leave it" associated with the "⊘" symbol at least four times. Be very careful at the beginning not to let your dog act inappropriately—stay close at hand so that he cannot misbehave. If you leave the room and he eats the treat out of the Kong, for example, the "⊘" symbol will lose its potency. As you strengthen his response to the sign, expand its use without reiterating the phrase "Leave it." If those results are satisfactory, begin to test it in circumstances that you are less able to monitor. If at any point he chooses to ignore the sign, revisit the training method again. Obviously, the stronger the temptation, the more likely he will want to ignore the symbol, so increase the temptation bit by bit.

Look, Ma, No Exercises!

*T*he ease with which your dog may read stick figures and symbols is a reward for the investment of time you have spent teaching her verbal commands and introducing her to flash cards with written words. Time and time again, I find dogs who can read stick figures with no training whatsoever! Some of my clients at the Assistance Dog Institute have had the same experience.

Hazel Weiss of Albany, California, has multiple sclerosis. Hams is her five-year-old golden retriever. Her first clue to his brilliance occurred at our institute, where she and Hams were learning to get in and out of an elevator together. Because of Hazel's MS, she tends to lose her balance. She remembers, "As we were getting out of the elevator, I stumbled to the left. Hams was at a *heel* position, and he stopped and pushed on my leg so that my hands rested on his shoulder. He was looking up at me like 'I've got you, it's okay.' "

He has since learned, when walking with Hazel, to slow down and get very close to her so that he can brace her whenever they are walking downhill.

In the three years since he has lived with Hazel, Hams has become a full-fledged companion and helpmate. In the morning, he brings her slippers to her bed ("Always two at a time, because he understands that they're a pair," she says), he puts her dirty laundry into the hamper, and he even transfers the clothes from the hamper to her front-loading washing machine. When the wash cycle is finished, he tugs the clothes out of the washer.

"Last October," Hazel continues, "I learned how to teach Hams to read. It really makes him smarter. It keeps him active, young, and thinking about things. Every time I teach him a new skill, he is ready to do more. Reading has added a quantum leap to his set of abilities."

It also makes him happy. "He loves to read! When I take out those flash cards, he starts wagging his tail and dancing around the room. Everything that makes Hams happy makes us both happy, and I think the more positive emotions we share, the healthier we are.

"When I saw my neurologist for a regular checkup a few months ago, he said, 'I think you're one of a small group of my patients who have taught your immune system not to attack itself.' Then, pointing to Hams, who was lying beside me, he added, 'And I think he probably has a lot to do with it.'

"I've had MS for fifteen years, and for the twelve years before I got Hams, my health was gradually declining. I have been stable for the last three years. His positive effect on me is totally linked to our relationship, and reading has contributed to that good relationship."

Hams is a fast learner. Before he began to read stick figures, he was a good reader of words and may have had as many as twelve words in his reading vocabulary.

Even though Hams clearly knew that he was expected to respond to a flash card, his ability to interpret a card with a stick figure with no exercises at all took everyone by surprise. "I was completely amazed, beside myself," Hazel says, "when I first held up the 'down' stick-figure card and he looked at me, looked at the card, nosed it, and he lay down!"

Sit is usually the first response for a dog, not down. When Hazel showed Hams the "down" card, he downed. He was standing, and he didn't go into a sit first—he looked at the card and he downed. For me this was absolutely conclusive—dogs can read and interpret stick figures without any prior teaching of stick figures! The screams of excitement that were coming out of that small room must have shook the whole school, because people from other classrooms hurried into the room.

Hazel continues, "After he had mastered *down* and *sit,* we moved on to *roll.* I backed up in my wheelchair, Hams moved toward me in a stand position, and I showed him the 'roll' card with no verbal cue at all. He looked at me and the card and went down. Then he looked at me as if to ask 'Is that good enough?' I replied, 'Nope.' And with an expression that said, 'Oh, okay, I'll roll then,' he rolled with lightning speed.

"Bonnie handed me the next card for *turn.* He looked at it and he turned. Then we tried the card for *up,* and he upped. Card after card, he continued to interpret the stick figure.

"When he's reading, I can see him figuring things out in a split second, and I *know* that he's stretching his mind—that he's really thinking. There's no limit to the implications of his ability to think for me. I know that if I'm in trouble, he will likewise figure out how to help me. I have total faith that he will use his intelligence to do whatever I need — like get the phone if I need help."

You may be teaching your own dog for the pure fun of it, or you, like Hazel, may be building your dog's brainpower because his help is indispensable to you. In the next chapter, we'll explore another one of the most practical contributions of reading dogs — helping children read.

Part iv

Reading Dogs
Go to
the Head
of the Class

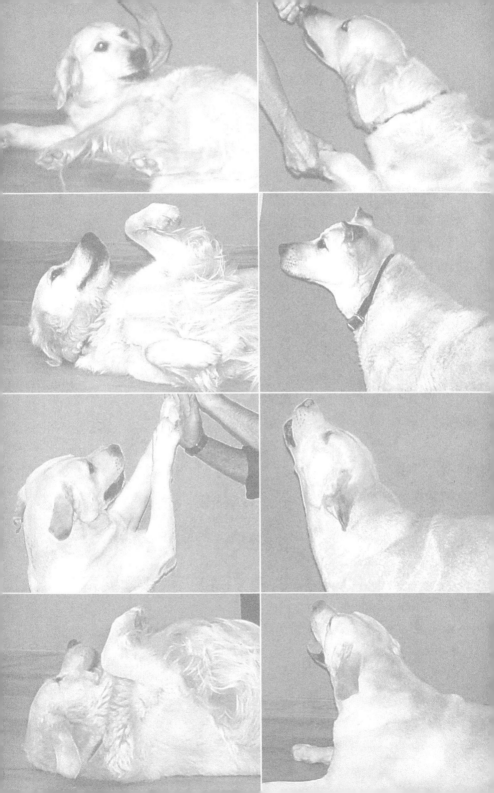

Chapter

7

Teach Your Dog
to Help Children
with Their Reading

*I*f you think teaching your dog to read has been a thrill, wait until you watch your reading dog help a child learn to read. For a child who is struggling, a visiting dog in the classroom transforms the experience of reading failure into one of fun and excitement. The reading environment becomes a dynamic stage on which a child can perform for an unconditionally loving being.

Dogs first took part in reading programs in schools in 1999 because of the work of a wonderful woman named Sandi Martin. She and her social/therapy dog Olivia volunteered in classrooms at Bennion Elementary School and held "dog day afternoons" at the Salt Lake Library in Salt Lake City, Utah. Children with reading difficulties had individual appointments to read to Sandi's dog.

The reading levels of children involved in these oral reading exercises skyrocketed. In less than a year, grade reading levels doubled and tripled. Impressive growth, thanks to Sandi and Olivia!

I was fascinated to hear of this development, and we invited Sandi to share her expertise at the Assistance Dog Institute's annual summer conference. Each year the conference focuses on the struggles of "at-risk" teens, gang life, and better ways to teach both kids and dogs. That fall and spring following Sandi's presentation, our college students began training their assigned dogs to read with children. For the next several months, we experimented and researched, expanding on Sandi's idea to create our program, "Opening DAORS" (Dog-Assisted Oral Reading System).

Reading is usually a quiet endeavor, so we taught our dogs to sit or lie quietly beside a person who was holding a book. Unfortunately, lying quietly for any length of time encourages snoozing. A dozing dog is obviously not being attentive to a child's oral reading. Worse, we were concerned that the child might emulate the dog's response!

So, we developed techniques to train the dogs in a *formal reading response*. In addition to a posture command like *sit* or *down*, we trained the dogs to respond to the command *read*. This command simply means to look at whatever reading material is present. Dogs can learn to respond to the command *read* by looking at a book as if they are absorbing the sonnets of Shakespeare!

In this chapter, you'll find our methods for training a dog to read with children. First, you will need to teach your dog to look at a book and respond to the command *read*. Then he will need to learn to move up next to a child and sit or lie down to become his or her reading buddy. I will also show you how your dog can become comfortable "reading" beside a child for long periods of time without your obvious direction and without the immediate gratification of treats.

In this secure environment, with the love and companionship of the dog, most children are delighted to read. You — the dog's owner or handler — will be right there to assist the child with any reading skills without making her feel ostracized or embarrassed about her reading ability.

The fact that your dog can read actual words — especially if he can read five or six words — makes him an even more dynamic reading companion. The child's motivation and excitement about reading will increase enormously. She will think, "If that dog can read, of course I can read!"

This chapter also includes ways in which you can:

- Decrease your dog's dependence on you so that he can bond with the child who needs some help with reading.
- Keep your dog well groomed and healthy, and teach him simple manners so that he can safely volunteer in a library or classroom.
- Respond to the reading dog and child in the most helpful way. One-on-one oral reading is a powerful tool for making children comfortable with the written word. Just being present as an adult, even on the pretext of accompanying a dog who is visiting the classroom, can help children become more at ease with oral reading.

Opening the First DAOR: Teach Your Dog to Look at a Book

To teach your dog to focus on a book as if she were really reading it, sit on the floor or on a short stool. Your dog should be beside or in front of you in a sit or down position. Have a nicely stocked treat bag readily available. The goal is to teach your dog to gaze at the book for a long time.

As you know, associations are learned in increments, bit

by bit. The first bit now is to get your dog to give the book a quick glance. Gradually you will help her to increase her glances into a lengthy stare.

For this exercise, you will need:

- Readily accessible treats (in a treat bag or on a nearby tabletop)
- A tiny squeak toy
- A clicker (if you use one instead of "Yes!")
- A picture book

You may need to teach this response over several days. If so, limit each day's adventure in reading to six to nine exercises.

Teach Your Dog to Look at a Book in Five Easy Steps

Step 1. Say "Read!"

While you are sitting down, hold a treat in your hand and make sure that your dog is at your side or in front of you. Give the command *read* and simultaneously reach around behind the book (if your dog is sitting beside you) or hold the treat behind the open book (if your dog is sitting in front of you). The split second that your dog tries to look *through* the open book, before he tries to push the book aside or nose behind it, give a "Yes!" (or click with a clicker) and bring the treat forward to give it to him along with praise and pets. You need to be fast to teach your dog that he will get the treat when he just looks at the book.

Repeat this step until your dog looks at the book without going nuts trying to chase down the treat behind it.

Step 2. Squeak!

*H*old the squeak toy behind the book. Now give the command *read* and *immediately* follow it with a squeak. Your dog's attention should be drawn to the page without that incessant drive to nose the book aside looking for food. When his ears, eyes, and body are directed to the reading material in front of the toy, follow with a timely "Yes!" or click and a treat, praise, and pets.

Step 3. Tap!

*N*ow your dog has the idea that looking at the page in response to the *read* command and a squeak cue results in a treat. We want to add another cue to those in his repertoire. Teaching him to respond to a target, like a tap on the book page, is a useful cue that a child can give if the dog's attention wanders. Situate your dog so that he is now looking at the

open book beside you. As soon as he shifts his gaze elsewhere, tap the book so that he redirects his attention to the book. Then reward him with a treat and praise.

Step 4. Cueless

*n*ext you'll take a small step so that your dog will look at the book without a physical cue—he will simply respond to the command *read*. Your goal is to have your dog respond to the word *read* without any physical cues whatsoever. His eyes and attention should shift to the reading material that you are holding. Begin by giving the *read* command. The split second your dog's head turns to the page, give a "Yes!" or a click followed by a treat, praise, and pets. Repeat this step until just speaking the word *read* will engage his attention.

Step 5. Hold It

*T*o increase the length of time your dog continues to look at a page, you'll use the same tricks that you used to teach him to extend his "up" (see p. 110). Again, work in tiny increments, bit by bit. The first step, as I mentioned above, is to get your dog to do what you want him to do. This behavior is followed by a marker—either "Yes!" or a click—that signifies that he has successfully completed the exercise. Reward his success with a treat, praise, and pets. To increase the length of time he maintains any posture is a simple matter of delaying the "Yes!" or click bit by bit.

When your dog truly understands the role of the "Yes!" or click as a marker, he will stay in that posture an extra millisecond or two waiting to hear it. He'll be on edge like a child waiting for the recess bell to ring. The more uncomfortable or purposeless the posture, the shorter time he will be willing wait.

Try to sense how long your dog can wait and delay the marker to that point, but not beyond it. One millisecond too long will result in the dog quitting on his own. Not only did he not wait—he now has learned to take the initiative to quit! This lesson, once learned, is very difficult to reverse.

As the saying goes, timing is everything. Think in terms of increasing his attentiveness time bit by bit, millisecond by millisecond. Build his ability to stay focused on the reading material by adding a millisecond each time before saying "Yes!"

ELIMINATE "YES!" AND TREATS

Now your dog thinks of the *read* command in much the same way as he does *down* and *roll*. When asked, he performs. It is no longer necessary to use markers like "Yes!" or clicks. They were used only to help guide his learning, to help him identify what you wanted when you wanted it—so that he might "get it." He now has it. It's a part of his repertoire.

It's also no longer necessary to give treats each time. Treats are always used following "Yes!" in the training phase. In the performance phase, they are used intermittently just to keep your dog interested.

Teach Your Dog to "Read" in All Kinds of Places

*I*t's now time to generalize your dog's response to the command *read*. Just as she responds equally well when asked to sit on carpet, linoleum, asphalt, or grass, so should she respond equally well when you ask her to read paper, tabloids, novels, and large and small picture books held by someone near her in different rooms and settings.

When you introduce your dog to reading, she needs your help to make the leap that *read* means *read* irrespective of the reading material, location, or people around her. To build these generalizations, you need to back up a step or two in her training. That means reintroducing the squeak toy, tapping, treats, and, yes, "Yes!"

She does not need to be introduced to every new location, every new person, or every different type of book or paper product in order to realize that the *read* command applies to each. That is the beauty of her prewired ability to generalize! You only need to teach her that *read* applies to two or three different situations. Her mind will do the rest. Let's begin with different types of reading materials.

1. Start with a new children's picture book, because this will be one of your more frequently used reading materials. Hold it open and place the squeak toy behind it.
2. Give the *read* command while almost simultaneously squeezing the toy.
3. The split second your dog shows interest in and looks at the book, say "Yes!" and give her a treat.

One or two run-throughs is generally all it takes for your dog to get the idea. Those numerous carefully handled steps used to teach the word *read* with that first picture book are now synthesized down to one or two exercises with a new picture book.

To further build the generalization, using a magazine, run through the same exercise. This time, eliminate the squeak toy. Simply tap the page a split second after you give the command *read*. This cue should suffice. Of course, if your dog does not respond correctly, it's possible that the initial *read* command was not as solid in her mind as it needs to be. Just back up and review the initial steps, starting with Step 1.

To generalize her reading to other rooms and locations, start with an entirely different room in your house. Get that first picture book and follow the steps outlined above. Use the squeak toy in the first exercise, followed by tapping in the second. Don't forget to reward her with "Yes!" and treats each time. Now go to a schoolroom or library and practice there, starting with that first picture book and adding others as your dog succeeds.

Teach Your Dog to Look at a Book with a Child

Generalizing the exercise to include other people takes a little more effort because you are bringing a third person into the equation. People volunteer with their dogs for love — theirs for their dog. They want to share that love, yet in some sense they want to keep it to themselves. I have seen hundreds of people do social/therapy work with their dogs. It is not unusual to see the dog owner/volunteer's arm draped over the dog or his or her hand unconsciously stroking the dog. He or she may also hold a conversation with the dog in front of the person they are visiting. That's not good manners! It's as if the volunteer is visiting with his own dog, not encouraging his dog to visit with others.

Undoubtedly one aspect of a social/therapy dog's role is to motivate his human partner to volunteer. It is so much easier and more enjoyable to go somewhere with your dog than to go alone. Dogs are social icebreakers. They invite smiles and interactions. And you have a friend, a true friend, with you at every moment.

That reassuring meeting of the eyes, the comforting presence of his body leaning against you, your fingers securely sifting through the hairs on his back are each a part of your own motivation to get up and go. Trying environments are transformed into warm, friendly places with your dog by your side.

Adults who read the body language message that the two of you come as a package (*love my dog, love me*) will be inclined to respond to that message. Kids may be more sensitive to your emotional need to keep your dog to yourself. That understanding may well be a disincentive for the child to engage with your dog. So, when you take your dog to a school or library to visit and read with a child, let your dog bond with her. Encourage, no—*train* your dog to move up next to the child and become her reading partner. Let the glow of love encompass the two of them in a reading exercise, while you linger on the periphery, supporting the exchange.

Most oral reading is done with kids and dogs lying together on the floor. You taught the *read* command to your dog while you and your dog were both sitting so that your arms were free to lure, target, treat, and pet. Now that your dog is successful at reading, you can teach him to read from either a sit or a down position.

TEACH YOUR DOG TO GET INTO READING POSITION

1. With your dog on a leash (he will need to be on leash in a school), lie on the floor. Give the *here* command while you point to a spot beside you. ("Here" is a wonderful command for any social/therapy work. Almost like the point and click with a computer mouse, you simply say "Here" and point, and your dog moves to that location.)

2. As your dog moves to the correct spot, follow the word *here* immediately with *sit* or *down*. Do not offer treats or

praise in between. If he circles and lies facing the wrong direction, tell him "No" and immediately get him up (or tell him to "turn."). Get up and move a step or two away while you call your dog to come to you. Repeat the sequence. Getting up and down could get old quickly, particularly if your body is old to start with. It will also tire your dog, who will try to pay more attention in order to solve the dilemma.

3. A dog's body follows his head, so if you continue having trouble with positioning his sit or down, the third or fourth time he sits or downs facing the wrong direction, firmly give the *here* command, tapping where you want his head to be. When he repositions himself, even if not perfectly, say "Yes!" and give him a treat, praise, and pets.

4. Repeat this exercise until he responds without prompting. Remember, six to nine repeats of the same exercise is about the upper limit for any one training session. If more practice is necessary, continue the next day. Don't burn your dog out in your determination to nail down this concept in one day.

TEACH YOUR DOG TO GET DOWN AND READ

Once your dog has learned how to position his body to be a reading buddy, add a book to the exercise as you incorporate the *read* command. Almost any time something changes in the learning context, be prepared to back up a step or two to recharge the exercise, teaching it again in the new context. If, when you say "Read," your dog doesn't immediately turn his head to the book you are holding, repeat the command while tapping a page with your finger. When your dog turns to look, say "Yes!," treat, praise, and pet.

TEACH YOUR DOG TO LIE DOWN AND READ WITH
A TRAINING PARTNER

Day One. Training your dog to read with someone eventually requires a someone to train with. You could, of course, start with a body pillow to teach your dog the correct position for reading. That might be of some help, but a real person will engender different reactions in your dog. It helps enormously to have a human partner in this effort before you go to a school.

1. Your human training partner should lie on the floor with a book in hand. Throughout this exercise, he or she should remain still.
2. Stand near but slightly in front of the spot where your dog is to lie down. Point to the spot and say "Here."
3. Once your dog moves to the correct spot, give the *down* command. Since you are slightly in front of your dog, he probably will lie down facing forward because he is used to aligning himself with your body. However, having another body in the mix—that of your training partner—makes this a new situation for your dog.

   If he circles and lies down facing the wrong direction, tell him "No," move a step or two away, and call him to you. Repeat the "here" and "down" sequence again. The likelihood that he will lie down facing away from where you are standing is slim; if he does make this mistake, it may be your positioning that needs adjusting. If you choose to lie down first, encourage him to join you and his reading partner. Be aware that he will probably align his body next to yours. You might want to wait until he is fully trained in reading with a partner before you lie down first.

4. Once he lies downs correctly, give a hearty "Yes!" followed by a treat, praise, and pets.
5. Repeat this exercise a few more times until your dog seems comfortable with the requirements.

Day Two. The next day, practice getting your dog into reading position with the *down* command again. If, as is so often the case, overnight learning solidified the lesson, move on. This next step involves your training partner giving the *read* command.

1. Dogs, like humans, do things for a reason. A dog will respond to a command because doing so is relevant to him. If someone is prepared to give him a treat, particularly a good treat, that makes it relevant! This exercise starts with your training partner giving your dog a treat or two to become *relevant* to your dog. Remain standing in a relaxed manner so as not to distract your dog. (It might help if your training partner directs your dog with "Here," then "Sit" or "Down," just to clarify her role in this exercise.)
2. After your partner lies down, your dog should be directed to lie beside her. When your dog is lying down, sit next to him or, better still, sit on the other side of your training partner. (This positions you perfectly to help a young reader, while your dog, on the other side, provides love and motivation.) Think of yourself as being invisible to your dog so that his entire concentration is on reading.
3. With her book in place, your training partner should tell your dog to "Read," tapping the page to underscore the command in this new context.
4. When your dog looks at the page, your training partner should give him a treat and praise him. (Since her timing

using "Yes!" may not be good, and your dog already knows the routine, praise and a treat should suffice.)

5. Repeat this exercise until you feel sure your dog is comfortable with the situation.

6. Refrain from touching, petting, draping your arms over him, or any other mannerism that spells out your need to be near your dog. Decrease your dependency on your dog and your dog's dependency on you. You are lending him out for this exercise. Take pleasure in his willingness to help a child improve her reading skills—he will take his cue from you. When you go to the library or school, encourage a child to touch, pet, and put her arm around your dog. Doing so will strengthen her communication and connection with your dog, thus increasing her motivation to read to him.

Get Your Dog Ready to Read with a Child

Once your dog is comfortable lying beside a reading partner, she can lie down and read with a child. However, before she can volunteer safely in a school or library and work with children, you need to make sure that she is healthy, clean, and well behaved.

FIT AS A FIDDLE

Your dog should have had a veterinary exam within the last year, and she should be current with all of her vaccinations. She should be free of both internal and external parasites, such as worms, fleas, and ticks. Nothing should be oozing from her skin, eyes, ears, or the area beneath her tail.

When you go to the school or library, take a copy of your dog's rabies vaccination certificate and other forms from your vet that show that your dog is in good health.

THE WELL-GROOMED GUEST READER

In addition to being healthy, make sure that your dog is a handsome visitor! To make her beautiful:

- Bathe her weekly or when needed with mild dog shampoo so that she's odor-free. Don't use a perfumed shampoo—some children may have allergies.
- Trim her nails and make sure that they are smooth.
- Brush her teeth every day. A battery-powered toothbrush can help to prepare your dog to deal with distracting noise and movement.
- Clean around (not in) the openings of her ears with a pH-balanced ear cleanser.
- Dress her up in a cape or a bandanna, or hang a pair of reading glasses around her neck to show that she is a reading star.

MANNERS MATTER

Being healthy and dressed for success are only two parts of the preparation equation. You also must consider your dog's demeanor before you take her into a room full of children. Obviously she should be kid-friendly and comfortable with all kinds of people.

I strongly recommend that you take your dog to a social/therapy dog course before you take her into a school or library. These courses differ from standard dog training classes in that they focus on dogs' behaviors in environments other than the home. Simple manners are a must, and your dog should be tested for any questionable behaviors. At the very least, your dog should understand that it's not kosher to pee or poop inside and that jumping up and nosing the teacher's crotch is taboo.

Other skills that your dog may need to work on may include:

- Not barking incessantly
- Not growling or barking at other dogs, kids, or adults or unusual wall hangings, balloons, or other sights and sounds
- Not pulling away or trying to avoid children
- Not trying to jump on or kiss kids
- Not begging if there are treats in the room

She should be able to:

- Stay under control without needing to be physically restrained while walking into unfamiliar, potentially distracting surroundings
- Ignore toys and food on the ground
- Handle exuberant petting and hugs
- Lie quietly for two to three twenty-minute intervals

To find a class in dog manners, contact an assistance dog program in your area (see www.adionline.org for listings). Therapy Dogs International and the Delta Society also offer courses (see the resources listed at the back of this book).

HOW OLD SHOULD THE CHILD BE?

Once your dog is clear about good manners and proper behavior with children, she is ready to visit a school. Reading dogs can contribute so much more than reading incentives when they go to school. For instance, in an elementary school in Stayner, Ontario, dogs have made reading fun for children by keeping them company while they read in the school library, resting their heads on the children's laps, retrieving the "reading" blanket and books, and walking the children back to their classes.

Elementary students clearly benefit from these visits, but

reading dogs can be helpful even to older students. I was pleasantly surprised when a team of college students from my Assistance Dog Institute took their reading dogs to a Catholic boys' home. There they read with eighth-grade students who were having reading difficulties. These teenagers, like the younger children whom we had more experience teaching, competed with each other for the opportunity to read to a dog.

At my institute, we also have found that teenagers who learn to teach dogs to read become better readers themselves. I've worked with many at-risk teens who have poor reading skills. Many assume there is no other way available to them than to follow in their parents' footsteps to jail, prison, drug and alcohol abuse, gangs, or burglary. Improving their reading abilities may help to expand their thinking, allowing them hope for other directions for their lives.

HOW OFTEN SHOULD I VISIT THE SCHOOL?

The number of visits you make to a school or library each week depends on the amount of free time you have available and your willingness to devote it to this effort. Two visits each week is a significant commitment. More than that could be overwhelming.

It is always better to do less and increase the frequency of your visits rather than to commit initially to more than you may enjoy. I've no doubt that as your visits inspire reading success, the teacher will seek more of your time. A teacher who is experienced will know not to push for fear of losing you altogether. I have seen many enthusiastic and eager volunteers burn themselves out in a matter of months. This is a case of the turtle beating the hare. For a long-term commitment, take it slow.

WHAT SHOULD I KNOW ABOUT WORKING IN SCHOOLS AND LIBRARIES?

For safety's sake, you must be able to control your dog at all times around children. Make sure that you have sound dog-handling skills, including training in targeting (pointing and tapping your finger) so that you can direct your dog as needed without pushing and pulling. You must have good communication with your dog.

You should also like children and have positive kid management skills!

Last, you'll need to be able to work well within the parameters of the school system.

Follow the rules. Learn the school/library policies, protocols, and expectations regarding volunteers and dogs. In turn, you should let the school and library staff know about the policies, protocols, and expectations of your reading dog program. You may, for instance, require a specific area for reading, and you may want to ask about the best area to take your dog outside if nature calls. Talk with the teacher or librarian ahead of time about your expectations of the children's behavior with respect to your dog's personality and your own. For instance, a high-strung dog and a high-strung child may not create the best reading partnership.

Stick to your schedule. You and your dog take this volunteer activity seriously, and you understand that a firm reliable schedule works best for the children. Be sure to tell the librarian or teacher that you will notify him or her of any days you will be unavailable well in advance. Get a copy of the school or library's master calendar (so you don't show up on a school holiday).

Do some dry runs. Visit the school or library *without* your dog to get the lay of the land and discuss how-tos with the powers that be. Discuss general safety around dogs, find out where the classroom and reading areas are, and ask and answer questions.

Next, go *with* your dog for a preliminary visit to get her familiar with the situation. Avoid crowds of children at the beginning and end of the school day and during recess times. If you visit the classroom where your dog will be reading, explain the purpose of today's visit to the children. While they remain seated, walk your dog around so that they can pet her. You can demonstrate your dog's ability to read, and if she knows any tricks, let her do a few. If she knows the commands, you can ask her to *bow* or *shake* when leaving.

HOW DOES A SCHOOL VISIT WORK?

It's your first day of taking your dog to read at school. You'll need more than sharp pencils and a new Snoopy lunch box to make this day go well. Here's what you should put in your backpack and what you should do when you enter the school.

What to bring with you. Water, a water bowl, and treats for your dog; a poop scoop kit; and disinfectant wipes for kids are essential. You may wish to bring some of your dog's reading flash cards as well as bookmarks with your dog's picture to give to the children. Also, if the children or their teacher or librarian have not selected a book to read to your dog (usually they have), you should bring along some books. Choose material that is appropriate to the children's reading level. Try to select books that are not too easy and not too hard—those that a child can read with about 90 to 95 percent accuracy. That means he or she should miss no more than ten words out of every hundred.

You might wish to select a book or two from the following list.

Entering the school. Now your books and backpack are ready to go. When you get to the school, remember to allow your dog to take care of business in the designated toilet area that you learned about on your preliminary visit. Be sure to clean up after her.

When you enter the school building, sign in (usually in the front office) to identify yourself as a visitor. Then walk to the classroom. Again, try to avoid visits to the school at the beginning and end of the day and during recesses, when the hallways may be packed with children.

When you enter the classroom, go directly to the reading area so you don't disturb classroom activities. If a reading specialist is available, talk with him or her about any directions.

CAUTIONS TO CONSIDER

Your visit to a school or library with your dog should be a safe, delightful experience for everyone. To keep it that way, always keep the following precautions in mind:

- Be prepared for potential disruptions. You might bring along a sandwich board sign with pictures or words that say "Team reading in session." Put the sign outside of the library or classroom or in front of that six-foot-square area assigned to you.
- Regularly monitor your dog's stress level.
- If you are sick or your dog is sick, forgo the visit that day.
- Do not let groups of children overwhelm your dog.
  - As you walk down hallways, keep your dog between yourself and the wall.

(continued)

- Allow only one or two children at a time to come near and pet your dog. Teach them how to pet and praise your dog.
- Encourage your dog to shake hands so he doesn't lunge forward to visit.
- Do not hand over your dog's leash to anyone other than his current reading companion (and even then, stay close at all times).
- If another dog is on site, do not let the dogs visit each other.
- Never, never, never leave your dog!
- Do not take pictures of the school, library, or children without permission.

Opening the Second DAOR: Prepare Yourself

Your dog is now ready to read with a child. Next *you* need to be trained. You are not a passive observer in this scenario. As the adult present, the child will look to you for help in reading, so your responses need to facilitate the process.

Consider the importance of reading out loud. One-on-one oral reading of and by itself is one of the strongest tools to improve a child's reading skill. Just being there, even on the pretext of bringing your dog in to the school or library to be read to, will make a difference. The primary worth of your visit comes from providing a context for a child to read.

Many poor readers come from families who have or use limited vocabularies. Just as a dog should know the spoken command before you teach him to read the word, a child needs to have heard and understood a spoken word before she is taught to read it. In some families, parents do not read stories to their children, nor do they encourage their children to read to them. In other homes, English may be the second language, and opportunities to learn vocabulary are limited. More than eight in ten kids in juvenile detention centers are illiterate. In part because of this dearth of strong reading skills, the United States puts 10 percent of our population in prisons. (Most developed countries incarcerate around 4 percent.)

In school, teachers have an enormous job to do. Keeping twenty or thirty energetic bodies and minds busy and interested in lessons is a nearly impossible job. Group oral reading exercises benefit the top students in the class, but less adept students may be embarrassed when they are compared to more capable readers in the group. Silent reading lacks the potential to correct mistakes and reinforce learning through interactive discussions.

Parents, peers, and volunteers can be as effective as teachers in guiding oral reading exercises. By volunteering to help children learn to read, you can truly make a difference. If you're shy, take your best friend along. It may take a village to raise a child, but if it takes your dog to get you into a classroom, take him with you!

HOW LONG SHOULD OUR READING SESSIONS BE?

A one-hour visit to a library or school is the norm. A thirty-minute session per child appears to be about the right amount of time for each lesson, so one hour would allow you to work with two children.

Generally that half-hour session is broken down into three parts. In the first five minutes, the child talks and plays with the

dog; the next twenty minutes are focused on reading, discussion, and rereading; and the last five minutes are devoted to closure.

The first five minutes. In the beginning of the session, you and your dog will meet and greet your student. The next time you work with this child, you can also show her how your dog can read and instruct her to teach your dog a new reading word using the methods described in Chapters 3 and 4.

The middle twenty minutes. Now it's time to settle down to reading. You will position your dog next to the child, who will be facing a book. Position yourself to see the book without interfering with the child and dog. Ask the child to read to your

dog. Use a reading approach that has been approved by a reading specialist (be sure to show him or her the suggestions in this book). Strive to keep the experience fun and on track, and help the child to be successful. End on a positive note by praising the student's reading. Point out something that your dog enjoyed (something the student did exceptionally well during this session).

The last five minutes. Say good-bye to the student and let the child say good-bye to your dog with a few minutes of dog-loving farewells. Check with the teacher or librarian to see if the child is allowed to give your dog a treat. If he or she agrees, show the child how to lay the treat on a flat hand and present it to your dog. Ask if you can give the child a memento, such as a bookmark with your dog's picture. The reading specialist may ask you to record the student's reading progress.

Dogs usually can manage to stay alert and attentive for these two thirty-minute sessions per day. More sessions are possible if the dog is older and more mature or has a long attention span; fewer sessions are better for younger dogs. Two thirty-minute sessions may seem short, but they prevent burnout.

Some teachers will ask you to do three sessions in an hour. Three twenty-minute sessions give more students an opportunity to read. You might try three sessions, if it doesn't shortchange the student and if you and your dog have the energy. Just make sure that you find the right balance so that when you leave the school, the children, your dog, and you will all be motivated to do it again!

CHILDREN AND DOGS AS READING PARTNERS

Oral reading was the mainstay of reading curriculums through the first decade of the twentieth century. The term *blab schools* humorously acknowledged the immense amount of reading aloud involved in lessons. With the advent of readily available reading material, however, silent reading was ushered in. The oral reading that was left in the curriculum often consisted of "round robin reading," or reading aloud by turns. This system had the unintended consequence of making poor readers stumble more while boring good readers to distraction. Neither form of reading was conducive to improved fluency and comprehension.

Today, new interest in oral reading has created an ideal environment for dog-assisted oral reading. The dog's presence transforms an association of reading with failure to an association of reading with fun and excitement.

Fired up about reading out loud. Children, just like dogs, need to be involved with sensory activities in the reading process. With the sights, sounds, and even doggy smells in the room, children's emotions will be heightened. Well-chosen questions about what the dog may be thinking about the story can add richness to the reading experience.

Again, just as with dogs, students do best when we present them with information that requires them to respond. We can elicit a response by exchanging questions about the reading material, discussing it, revisiting parts of it, speculating on the dog's perspective of it, and summarizing it for the dog (if she dozed through part of it). Working with the material in this way helps improve the child's performance on standardized tests.

How each dog can help most successfully has to do with you, your dog, and the environment. Obviously your activities cannot disrupt others, but vivid images and experiences do make a difference. Physical movements, emotional exchanges, and new ideas reinforce reading comprehension.

Once you have a few books to choose from, you'll need to consider the best way to help the child benefit from his reading session with your dog. Here are some possibilities. To strengthen the child's sensory response to the dog's presence, ask the child to:

- Draw pictures of certain scenes in the story that include the dog.
- Act out one of the scenes to help the dog better understand it.
- Retell a simplified version of the story to the dog.
- Choose words from the text (such as *sit, down,* and *shake*) that the dog really knows how to read. Using flash cards, show the child how the dog can read the words.
- Teach the dog a new word from the story.
- Think up questions about a book that a dog might ask if she could speak.
- Trace one of the written flash-card commands or stick-figures onto a separate sheet of paper. (This project could help your student develop letter and word recognition along with scanning left to right ability.)

What a difference your dog and you can make!

The rewards of reading. During the reading session, when you sense that the child can use a bit of encouragement, I highly recommend using "Yes!" to praise him; creating opportunities to pet your dog; and even allowing the child to

give your dog treats (if the teacher allows it). As in dog training, the point is to create a bond and to intensify significant increments in learning to reinforce memory.

If children are allowed to give your dog treats, limit food treats to the beginning or end of each session, perhaps when you use flash cards to demonstrate your dog's reading exercises.

Speaking of treats, how can you reward your dog for his efforts during these reading sessions? In schools and libraries, you want your dog to respond to the child, not look to you for direction and treats. Allowing the child to give the treats also can present a problem. Not only might it divert everyone's attention from reading, but treats can be messy and greasy, a poor combination with books.

For that reason, physical cues such as targeting (pointing to the book) are vital. They fit perfectly with reading because many children point to words or follow a line with their finger as they are reading. Cues like finger-tapping make use of the dog's natural response to sound and movement and make his reading response more reliable. Although occasional food treats will, like any intermittent reinforcement, refocus his efforts, targeting, praise, and petting may make food rewards unnecessary.

Using DAORS to Open More Doors

*T*he dog-assisted oral reading system (DAORS) includes five reading methods:

1. **Repeated reading:** The child reads the same passage out loud several times with guidance and feedback. Then we ask him to read the passage again so that the dog can understand the story better.
2. **Paired reading:** You and the child read the book together while the dog looks at the book with you.
3. **Echo reading:** The child reads a sentence after you read it; the dog is impressed.
4. **Alternate line reading:** You read the first sentence, the child reads the second sentence, and so on; the dog observes.
5. **Modeling reading:** You read aloud to the child and the dog.

Let's look at these methods more closely.

Repeated reading. A child's fluency improves as he reads the same passage out loud over and over again while you provide guidance and feedback. Although speed and accuracy will obviously improve with rereading, this fluency also transfers to other reading materials.

Repeated reading also gives the child enough familiarity with the material to transition from a word-by-word reading approach to reading phrases. In repeated readings, he can add inflections and changes in intonations better suited to the material. His increased proficiency also will add to his enjoyment—perhaps the most important goal of any reading program.

Oral reading and rereading deserve your time and attention. If your student objects or resists, try involving your dog. Tell the child you'd like the story read again to help the dog understand it better. Encourage him to reread a phrase that the dog might like to hear again. (Take care not to emphasize the words the dog knows as commands so she doesn't feel called on to respond.) Next, ask the student to reread the passage, pointing out to the dog words she knows as commands; either ask or don't ask her to respond. Ask the child to read with strong, clear intonations and inflections to help keep your dog awake and interested.

Paired reading. Paired reading is a hugely successful way to improve general reading performance. Here you join your student in the reading exercise, but she remains in control. Read the material aloud with the child—taking care to match her pace. Her finger needs to follow along the reading so that you can keep up. Have one prearranged signal that will allow her to tell you when she wants to go it alone and another for when she wants you to join in. The flow of the reading should not be interrupted, so a hand signal works best.

This is not the time to teach pronunciation or vocabulary. Just say the word correctly, perhaps even have the child repeat it correctly, and move forward. If the student gets stuck on a part of the reading, jump in without invitation. Read more loudly than she does when these rough spots occur; otherwise try to match her volume.

Students make more progress when they understand the

purpose of the exercises, so be sure to tell your student the ground rules for paired reading ahead of time. That way, she will be prepared and comfortable with your involvement. You might set it up so that both of you are reading to your dog.

Echo reading. Echo reading is another oral reading exercise that involves you in the reading scheme. This time, you start as the lead reader. Read a sentence; then your student should reread that *same* sentence. You are modeling good reading for him, helping him learn to read by phrases instead of word by word. However, when he rereads the material, he should follow it along with his finger. He should be reading the words, not just repeating yours.

At some point, during this session or another, your student can become the lead reader with you doing the "echo."

Alternate line reading. Alternate line reading is similar to echo reading, but without the echo. Instead, you and the child take turns reading one or two sentences each. Your involvement in echo and alternate line reading increases your student's enjoyment of reading by including both of you without the intensity of paired reading. These should be happy, fun, but engaging exercises.

Modeling reading. Here again you are involved in the reading session, this time as the sole reader. Some of the best moments students experience in school occur when their teachers read to them.

Reading aloud to a child serves several purposes. First and foremost, it promotes her desire to read. It also excites her to see you emotionally moved by the reading material. She now has an opportunity to hear fluent reading in a

Most children will never forget a dog's visit to their classroom or library. To make the experience even more memorable, you can:

- Make bookmarks with each child's name and a picture of your dog.
- Teach your dog to carry a lightweight lunch box, small backpack, or book in his mouth.
- Dress your dog in festive costumes on holidays.

voice that expresses the emotions and actions of the story. If you select the reading material and you choose something that is unfamiliar to the student (with the teacher's approval), she will be exposed to a wider field of interest. You can also choose material that is somewhat above the student's reading level, so it can be rich with stimulating vocabulary and sentence structures.

Use Your Dog to Help Children Correct Their Reading Errors

*W*ith a dog at your side, you can gently encourage children to become better readers by working on words that are new or difficult for them.

SOUNDING OUT WORDS

If you need to help a younger child with a word, point to each letter and *say the sound made by each letter in that specific word.* Then have him repeat the sounded-out word to the dog. *Do not* say the letter name of the letter, and *do not* suggest that those same letters make those same sounds in other words. The sounds of the letters of the alphabet do not correspond to their use in most words, and letter combinations can and do have different sounds in different words. Many of us were taught reading with techniques that are faulty. Let's *not* pass them on.

VOCABULARY BUILDING

In dog training, intensity helps the dog learn. In vocabulary building, vivid images related to the word help the child learn. Repeated exposure to a word through your rereading exercises followed by discussion helps teach a child a new word. So does your introduction of and use of the word before the reading exercise (if you know which word will be difficult ahead of time).

Two other methods have good results with poor readers. First, when a child encounters a difficult or unknown word, you can substitute a simpler, more readily understood synonym for it (for example, *dog* for *canine*). Second, without allowing her to feel a sense of failure, encourage the child to search for clues in the story or accompanying pictures to figure out the unknown word. Provide the definition of the word before she gets discouraged.

Tying a new vocabulary word to an exercise that includes the dog is another great way to reinforce words. If you modeled an emotion described in the reading, your dog would likely react emotionally in response. If you act out a scene from the story with your dog, you would certainly cause a stir. If your reading exercises are taking place in a classroom with other children, you could do the action in slow motion to avoid disrupting the entire class.

Both dogs and children learn to read best when the experience is intensified by pleasure. There are endless possibilities for you and your dog to bring pleasure to a child who is learning to read. I hope you will send some of your own ideas to me so that I can run them past reading experts and disseminate them to others. The e-mail address is: openingdaors@ assistancedog.org.

The field of dogs reading—and children reading to dogs— needs to expand. Your participation in this process is essential as an advocate, a dog parent and partner, a dog lover, an innovator, and an implementer. Amazing lessons await you, your dog, and some lucky children—you just need to open the "daors"!

Chapter

8

Take Part in the Reading Revolution

The Potential of Dogs Is Beyond Words!

*W*hen children are taught to read early, their ability to conceptualize expands. In humans, the networking of four different parts of the brain in order to read creates mental abilities that have led to significant scientific advancements. We don't know what parts of the dog's brain connect in reading, but we're teaching dogs to read so that they will be better able to solve problems for people. And the younger we start teaching them, the more they seem to grasp.

Where will our reading dogs lead us? At the Assistance Dog Institute, we're exploring a lot of different avenues.

READING DOGS IN RESEARCH

We know that dogs have a phenomenal ability to sniff odors. Their olfactory system is far superior to ours — so much so that they can sniff out drugs in baggage areas of airports and help search and rescue teams locate people in rough terrain and in water.

Dogs, by scent, also can identify bladder, prostate, ovar-

ian, and breast cancer cells from urine samples in petri dishes. We're looking at teaching very young dogs to read so that as they mature, they will have greater reliability when they sniff a petri dish and then select a specific cancer from a series of flash cards on the wall (the cards would spell out "bladder," "prostate," "ovarian," "breast," or "nothing" if they

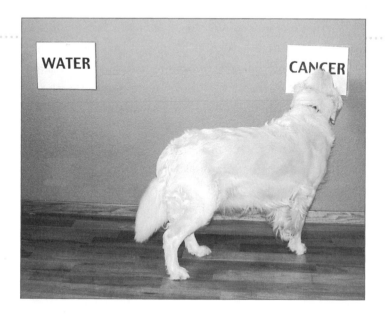

do not detect any cancer). In the same way, they can also tell us if a person with diabetes has low blood sugar.

READING DOGS IN SPACE AND TIME

In addition to their potential as teachers and researchers, we're exploring ways in which reading dogs can conceptualize and comment on the world. Children need to learn spatial, time, and object awareness in order to manage in the world. We suspect that the same is true of dogs. At three or four weeks of age, they will walk right off a table edge. Over time, they develop a better sense of space and understand that a table ends and, if they step over the edge, it's a quick drop to the floor.

But who is teaching them to count and to identify and communicate concepts like rough and smooth, round and square, and black and white to us? With a strong communication system based on a written vocabulary, just how much deeper will our relationship be with our dogs? If we say the word *round*, for instance, they can go to a round object to show us that they understand. If they, in turn, want to tell us that something is hot or cold, they can communicate with us by going to cards that contain those words. Our dogs are already so good at understanding us; reading would provide a way for us to understand them, too.

We also know that dogs have a strongly developed concept of time. My dogs line up at exactly 6 P.M. every weekend day staring at me, nudging me, barking at me with the clear message that it is time for their evening treat. We can teach a dog to nudge an older person to ask for a treat at a certain time every day. The nudge will remind the older person that it's time not just for the dog's treat, but for his or her pills, too. As I age, I am becoming more aware every day of the need for a supplemental memory system. Dogs who learn more strategies to communicate with us can become increasingly more helpful to humans.

The possibilities of reading dogs are endless. We just need to keep exploring them. One of the most exciting consequences of a dog's ability to read is this potential to enhance the system of communication between dogs and people. Dogs watch our body language, listen to our words, and are attentive to and perceptive to their environment and us, but we are not as attentive to and aware of them. We don't have to be—because they are so attuned to us already.

But what if we posted words such as *water* and *toilet* so that they could nose a flash card to communicate their needs and desires to us? What if we could establish a form of communication that we've never had before? As I explained in Chapter 6, if we teach dogs the symbol for *no* ("⊘") and that the symbol means "absolutely do not do whatever you were thinking of in relationship to this item," then very likely we could post a "⊘" card in front of a steak on the counter. It would serve as an ongoing reminder—much more powerful than a single verbal command that you said just before you left but which evaporated into thin air as soon as your body left the premises.

How Is Your Dog Reading?

*A*t the Assistance Dog Institute, which is dedicated to helping dogs help people, we are learning more every day about how dogs can read and think. The stick-figure exercises have shown us just what intelligent, cognizant beings they are. New research also suggests that their ability to respond to photographs—to understand the symbolism of an image that looks real—stems from a very sophisticated thought process.

I overlooked the true implication of a dog's ability to read photographs. In those initial experiments in teaching dogs to read, I showed Keila and Nexus 8½ x 11-inch photographs of other dogs sitting, downing, and rolling. Both dogs looked at the photographs, then responded as though the photographs were visual commands. Unaware of the significance of their ability to take their cues from photos, I moved on to experiments with stick figures. I naively assumed that reading stick figures would require a greater cognitive capability than reading photographs.

I was wrong. According to University of Virginia researcher Judy DeLoache and her collaborators, a human infant in the first year of life responds to a photograph of an object as if it were real, grabbing at a picture of a spoon, for example. My dogs, however, responded with a more advanced level of visual comprehension. Shown a photographic image of a dog in a specific posture, they grasped its symbolic significance, and responded to it as a command they were required to perform. It remains to be seen how much further this aspect of dogs' intelligence can be taken.

I hope that this book will inspire you not just to teach your own dog to read, but to put his reading skills to work in novel and helpful ways. The institute, in conjunction with the Assistance Dog United Campaign (ADUC), is offering a $1,000 annual Innovations in Dogs' Reading Award. Please contact us about the astounding things that your reading dog can do.

For more information and to apply for this award, contact:

The Bonnie Bergin Assistance Dog Institute
1215 Sebastopol Road
Santa Rosa, CA 95407
e-mail: info@assistancedog.org
website: assistancedog.org

Reading dogs are revolutionaries—and by teaching them to be literate beings, we can participate in their revolution. We can take them forward in their development at least twenty words beyond where they've ever been!

Now that you've taught your dog to read, share this book with a friend. Spread the word that anyone can help a dog become a smarter, better companion by building his mind through reading. Although it's amazing, when you teach a dog to read, you're not just teaching him a cute trick to show your friends. You're doing much, much more: You're developing his mind and helping him to become a better problem solver. My wish is that this book of simple training techniques will transform your expectations about what your dog can learn and do at home, and it will change the way that vets, dog trainers, and breeders approach dog training forever.

Resources

Flash cards of words and stick figures can be downloaded from: www.assistancedog.org/readingdogs.

Sponsors of reading programs in schools, libraries, youth clubs, and juvenile detention centers:

- American Kennel Club's Canine Good Citizen Test, akc.org
- Assistance Dog Institute's K-9 Support Program, assistancedog.org
- Assistance Dog International, Inc. (a coalition of organizations and individuals who train and place assistance dogs); Standards for Training Social/Therapy Dogs, adionline.org/therstand.html
- Delta Society, Renton, WA, deltasociety.org
- Intermountain Therapy Animals, Reading Education Assistance Dogs (READ) program, UT, therapyanimals.org
- Therapy Dogs, Inc., therapydogs.com
- Therapy Dogs International, tdi.org

Recommended Reading

Abrantes, Roger. *Dog Language: An Encyclopedia of Canine Behavior.* Wenatchee, WA: Dogwise Publishing, 2001.

Beck, Alan, and Aaron Katcher. *Between Pets and People: The Importance of Animal Companionship.* Bloomington, IN: Purdue University Press, 1996.

Becker, Marty. *The Healing Power of Pets: Harnessing the Ability of Pets to Make and Keep People Happy and Healthy.* New York: Hyperion, 2002.

Burch, Mary R. *Volunteering with Your Pet: How to Get Involved with Animal-Assisted Therapy with Any Kind of Pet.* New York: Howell Book House, 1996.

———. *Wanted: Animal Volunteers.* New York: Howell Book House, 2002.

Davis, Kathy Diamond. *Therapy Dogs: Training Your Dog to Help Others,* 2nd ed. Wenatchee, WA: Dogwise Publishing, 2002.

Fine, Aubrey, ed. *Handbook on Animal-assisted Therapy: Theoretical Foundations and Guidelines for Practice.* San Diego, CA: Academic Press, 2000.

Fogle, Bruce. *Pets and Their People.* New York: Viking Press, 1984.

The International Reading Association's Summary of the National Reading Panel Report, "Teaching Children to

Read" (Washington, DC: U.S. Department of Health and Human Services, 2000).

Reid, Pamela. *Excel-erated Learning: Explaining in Clear English How Dogs Learn and How Best to Teach Them.* Berkeley, CA: James & Kenneth Publishers, 1996

Ruckert, Janet. *The Four-footed Therapist: How Your Pet Can Help You Solve Your Problems.* Berkeley, CA: Ten Speed Press, 1987.

Index